SOCIETY FOR NEW TESTAMENT STUDIES

MONOGRAPH SERIES

General Editor: R. McL. Wilson, F.B.A.
Associate Editor: M. E. Thrall

35

PAUL: CRISIS IN GALATIA

A Study in Early Christian Theology

Paul: crisis in Galatia

A Study in Early Christian Theology

GEORGE HOWARD

Professor of Religion
University of Georgia

CAMBRIDGE UNIVERSITY PRESS

CAMBRIDGE

LONDON · NEW YORK · MELBOURNE

Published by the Syndics of the Cambridge University Press
The Pitt Building, Trumpington Street, Cambridge CB2 1RP
Bentley House, 200 Euston Road, London NW1 2DB
32 East 57th Street, New York, NY 10022, USA
296 Beaconsfield Parade, Middle Park, Melbourne 3206, Australia

First published 1979

Printed in Great Britain by
Redwood Burn Ltd
Trowbridge and Esher

Library of Congress Cataloguing in Publication Data
Howard, George, 1935–
Paul: Crisis in Galatia.
(Society for New Testament studies monograph series; 35)
Bibliography: p.
Includes index.
1. Bible. N.T. Galatians - Criticism, interpretation, etc.
I. Title. II. Series: Studiorum Novi Testamenti Societas.
Monograph series; 35.
BS 2685.2.H68 227'.4'06 77-84002
ISBN 0 521 21709 1

To my parents
F. S. and Ann Howard

CONTENTS

PREFACE

The present study is a re-evaluation of Paul's letter to the Galatians, and, with the exception of a few references to Romans, 1 Corinthians, and Acts, is confined almost exclusively to Galatians. This means that a great many problems in current New Testament studies, particularly those involving the relationship of Paul's letters with Acts, are avoided. This is the case for two reasons: (1) the issue of the relationship of Paul's letters with Acts takes us far beyond the scope of the present work and is reserved for a later time; (2) in the judgment of the writer many of the problems arising from this relationship are caused by a misunderstanding of Galatians. The present study aims at re-examining the traditional interpretations of this letter and proposes a re-interpretation of it. As a result a few suggestions for re-evaluating the relationship of Paul's letters with Acts are given; but these are only provisional and programmatic.

The title of the study, *Paul: Crisis in Galatia. A Study in Early Christian Theology*, indicates my method of approaching Pauline theology. It suggests that Paul's genius is seen best when his theology is allowed to arise from the historical setting of his struggles with opponents and his methods in preaching the gospel. An understanding of Paul's theology and biblical historical exegesis go hand in hand. It is the historical exegetical process which must come first if there is to be a genuine understanding of Paul's theology. The present study is a historical exegetical approach to Galatians which concludes with certain (though by no means all) theological insights into Pauline thought.

There are two conclusions which arise from this study, which, though historical in nature, are not argued for or even systematically examined. It is best simply to state them at the beginning. (1) Galatians is held to be very early and is probably the earliest letter of Paul extant. (2) The meeting between Paul, Peter, James, and John, recorded in Gal. 2: 1-10, is not equated with the Jerusalem Conference recorded in Acts 15. The flow of the discussions throughout the book demands these conclusions.

The writer owes much to his predecessors. This is especially true in regard to those with whom he often disagrees. Much of what he writes has been provoked by those whose conclusions are farthest from his own. For this reason he has a feeling of close kinship with all who have studied Galatians regardless of their conclusions.

A special debt of gratitude is owed to Dr Robert Ayers and Dr John McRay who read the manuscript in draft form and made many helpful suggestions for its improvement. Any errors that remain are, of course, mine, not theirs. Appreciation is also extended to Mrs Lucile Epperson who proofread the final copy.

November 9, 1976   *George Howard*
                                                                                  University of Georgia

ABBREVIATIONS

ABR	*Australian Biblical Review*
BJRL	*Bulletin of the John Rylands Library*
BLE	*Bulletin de Littérature Ecclésiastique*
BR	*Biblical Research*
CBQ	*Catholic Biblical Quarterly*
CP	*Classical Philology*
ET	*The Expository Times*
ETR	*Études Théologiques et Religieuses*
HTR	*Harvard Theological Review*
JBL	*Journal of Biblical Literature*
JR	*Journal of Religion*
JSJ	*Journal for the Study of Judaism*
Kaige	A recension of the Septuagint
KUD	*Kerygma und Dogma*
LXX	Septuagint
MT	*Masoretic Text*
MTZ	*Münchener Theologische Zeitschrift*
NT	*Novum Testamentum*
NTS	*New Testament Studies*
RHPR	*Revue d'Histoire et de Philosophie Religieuses*
RSR	*Recherches de Science Religieuse*
RSV	*Revised Standard Version*
SE	*Studia Evangelica*
SEA	*Svensk Exegetisk Arsbok*
TDNT	*Theological Dictionary of the New Testament.* Edited by G. Kittel and G. Friedrich. Translated by G. W. Bromiley. Grand Rapids, 1964.
TL	*Theologische Literaturzeitung*
TQ	*Theologische Quartalschrift*
TR	*Theologische Rundschau*

Abbreviations

TU	*Texte und Untersuchungen zur Geschichte der altchristlichen Literatur*
ZNW	*Zeitschrift für die neutestamentliche Wissenschaft*
ZTK	*Zeitschrift für Theologie und Kirche*

1

PAUL'S OPPONENTS IN GALATIA

I

Modern Pauline studies began with the Tübingen scholar, F. C. Baur.[1] In 1831 he published his 'Die Christuspartei in der korinthischen Gemeinde, der Gegensatz des petrinischen und paulinischen Christenthums in der ältesten Kirche, der Apostel Petrus in Rom.',[2] in which he first articulated his thesis that primitive Christianity was characterized by a conflict between Petrine and Pauline factions. Starting from 1 Cor. 1: 11–12, which delineates parties of those who followed Paul, Apollos, Cephas, or Christ, he argued that in reality there were only two parties, that of Peter which included the party of Christ and that of Paul which included the party of Apollos. The former group was the Jewish Christian Church which differed from Judaism proper mainly in that it accepted Jesus as the Messiah. It was this group that founded the church in Rome, opposed Paul at Corinth and Galatia, later came to be known as the Ebionites and was considered heretical by the church writers of the post-apostolic period. An important witness to Petrine Christianity, according to Baur, is the Pseudo-Clementine writings which record a struggle between Peter and Paul, who in these writings is camouflaged as Simon Magus.[3]

Baur's thoughts on Paul came to full fruition in 1845 when he published his now famous *Paulus*.[4] Using tendency criticism (i.e. criticism which noted the tendency in some documents to eliminate or play down the faction between Petrine and Pauline Christianity and thus to reflect the spirit of a later period), he acknowledged only Romans, 1 and 2 Corinthians and Galatians as genuine Pauline letters. In these he could see most clearly the conflict between the Petrine and Pauline factions. The other Pauline letters were written later when an attempt was being made to conciliate the two groups. The Acts of the Apostles was dismissed as historically unreliable in that it was an attempt by a Paulinist to bring about a rapprochement between the opposing groups by representing Paul as Petrine as possible and Peter as Pauline as possible.

In regard to Galatians Baur contended that the Apostolic Council, recorded in Gal. 2, had to do not merely with the opposition of the false brethren but with the Jerusalem apostles. 'The course of the transactions shows in what relation the Apostles stood with regard to the principles of these false brethren. They are themselves the opponents against whom the Apostle contends in refuting these principles.'[5] But the apostles were unable to withstand the power of Paul's defense and reasoning and acknowledged his independence, although full reconciliation did not ensue. An agreement was reached that Paul would go to the Gentiles and the Jerusalem apostles would go to the Jews; but this was merely a concession on the part of the latter not to oppose Paul. They themselves, while passive toward Paul's mission, remained in close connection with the zealous members of the Jewish Christian community who were consistent in their teaching that the law was necessary for salvation. Paul's opponents reflected in his letter to the Galatians, according to Baur, were these zealous Jewish Christians who, unopposed by the Jerusalem apostles, infiltrated his churches in order to complete the work of conversion by imposing on the Gentiles the requirements of the law.

By the end of the nineteenth century Baur had lost most of his followers.[6] Nevertheless, today the position which Baur articulated continues to play an important role in Pauline studies in general and Galatian studies in particular. Primarily it provides a base for modification or rejection. In the following pages we will attempt to give a representative (though not complete) survey of research in Galatians since the time of Baur[7] dividing the works into (1) those which view the opponents as Jewish Christian judaizers from Jerusalem and (2) those which do not. We will then set forth our own position, which is that the opponents were Jewish Christian judaizers supported by the apostles at Jerusalem. Our position differs from that of Baur in that, unlike Baur, it contends that the judaizers believed that Paul, like them, taught the necessity of circumcision and the law for salvation and were totally unaware of his non-circumcision gospel. This, as we will show in Chapter 2, is because Paul had just recently told the apostles of his revelation of a non-circumcision gospel to the Gentiles, and an insufficient time had elapsed for them to make the Jewish church aware of this new development in the Gentile mission.

The Galatian opponents: Jewish Christian judaizers from Jerusalem

In 1865 J. B. Lightfoot produced a commentary on Galatians in which he attempted to expose the fallacy of Baur's thesis.[8] He rejected Baur's contention that Acts was written in order to smooth over difficulties between Peter and Paul. He offered lengthy discussions showing how Acts and the autobiographical sections of Galatians harmonize. Moreover, he denied the Pseudo-Clementine writings as representing the true picture of the relationship between the two apostles. Rather its author used Peter as a mouthpiece for his own views. Likewise much of the post-apostolic literature about James and the Jewish church reflected a confused picture of the true situation.

As for Paul's relationship with the three, it was one of complete mutual recognition. The opponents of Paul in Galatia were Jewish judaizers probably from Jerusalem who may even have been followers of Christ himself. But they were not supported by the apostles. If the apostles were slow in checking the judaizers it was probably because they had hopes of conciliating them. As for James, Lightfoot conceded that he may have been in a slightly different situation from Peter, John, and Paul. These were required to become all things to all men, but James, as the local leader of the Jerusalem church, was required only to be a Jew to the Jews.

> But on the least favourable supposition it amounts to this, that St James, though he had sanctioned this emancipation of the Gentiles from the law, was not prepared to welcome them as Israelites and admit them as such to full communion: that in fact he had not yet overcome scruples which even St Peter had only relinquished after many years and by a special revelation; in this, as in his recognition of Jesus as the Christ, moving more slowly than the Twelve.[9]

In 1959 H. J. Schoeps[10] argued, against Baur and the Tübingen school, that there was no great gulf between Paul and the 'pillar' apostles. He rejected the late Pseudo-Clementine writings as being biased and unhistorical (though earlier he had considered them of more value). He saw the Galatian crisis in light of three positions: (1) Paul's, (2) Peter's and James', and (3) the judaizing extremists'. Schoeps argued that while we cannot take the account of Acts wholesale, since it dilutes the problems between Peter, James, and Paul, it is still clear that the former two took a moderate position at the Jerusalem Conference. Though at heart they may have inclined toward the more Jewish position, they made concessions to the Gentile mission and came to a mutual agreement with Paul.

As for the Galatian crisis itself the Jerusalem extremist group had infiltrated Paul's churches and taught that circumcision and the law were necessary for salvation. Their converts, 'those who accept circumcision' (Gal. 6: 13), had fanned the flames of Judaism and had caused great concern to Paul. But in no way were the 'pillar' apostles themselves instigators of this disturbance, nor were the judaizing extremists in any way their messengers. Schoeps says:

> The Tübingen conception of a deep gulf between Paul, on the one

hand, and James and Peter, on the other, which Baur, Schwegler, Volckmar, Hilgenfeld and their followers conjured up on the basis of the biased Jewish–Christian writings of the next generation, does not stand the test of impartial examination, and cannot possibly have reflected the real historical situation. Such a gulf is true only of the Pharisaic group of Judaizing Christians who were probably strongly represented in Jerusalem.[11]

Recently, Robert Jewett offered an explanation of the opponents in Galatia on the basis of an historical situation which had arisen in Judea.[12] The situation was the Zealot movement in the period leading up to the Roman war but especially during the procuratorship of Ventidius Cumanus (A.D. 48–52). During this time the Zealots sought to cleanse the Land of Israel of all Gentile elements in the hope that God would usher in the kingdom. They believed that God's wrath would be upon them until absolute separation from the heathen world took place. Zealot attention thus was directed against Gentile sympathizers like Paul (Acts 23: 12–22, 20: 3) and against all those connected with them (therefore a possible explanation for the persecution mentioned in 1 Thess. 2: 14–16). Jewett says:

> My hypothesis therefore is that Jewish Christians in Judea were stimulated by Zealotic pressure into a nomistic campaign among their fellow Christians in the late forties and early fifties. Their goal was to avert the suspicion that they were in communion with lawless Gentiles. It appears that the Judean Christians convinced themselves that circumcision of Gentile Christians would thwart Zealot reprisals.[13]

It was about this time that agitators first appeared at Antioch (Acts 15: 1–5) and sometime later at Galatia.

According to Jewett, the strategy of the judaizers was not to oppose Paul or his theology directly but to offer a perfection of it. 'The promise of perfection would have a powerful appeal to the Hellenistic Christians of Galatia, for such was the aim of the mystery religions as well as of classical philosophy.'[14] Circumcision and the cultic calendar as a means to this perfection would be most intriguing to the Galatians. But so as not to weaken their case the agitators did not mention that they were obliged to keep the whole law. Meanwhile the Galatians, with their pagan background, were as susceptible to libertinism as to Judaism. Consequently, since they believed that the Spirit gave them immediate immortality, they showed little interest in ethical distinctions.

The Galatian opponents: other than Jewish Christian judaizers from Jerusalem

In 1929 James Hardy Ropes published a monograph entitled *The Singular Problem of the Epistle to the Galatians*, which was a theory about the Galatian opponents based on an earlier work by Wilhelm Lütgert.[16] Ropes rejected the common view that the opponents were Jewish judaizers on the basis of Paul's arguments. He noted that though Paul argued for the futility of the law, he wished to retain contact with the Hebrew tradition as being essential to the gospel of Christ, a position which apparently did not belong to the opponents. He noted that the common view had the opponents appeal to the authority of the Jerusalem apostles against Paul and at the same time accuse him of being dependent on the Jerusalem apostles. He also argued that the common view did not fit in with the ethical section of the epistle which seemed to be 'a straightforward warning against lax tendencies, addressed to persons who really needed it'.[17] Ropes doubted that such a warning would have been addressed to judaizers who were trying to force people to keep the law.

Consequently, Ropes, following Lütgert, suggested as an alternate theory that the opponents actually belonged to two groups, each of which emphasized one side of Paul's teaching. One was a Gentile judaizing group which exaggerated the Hebraic element in Paul's doctrine and taught that the law was necessary to salvation. The other was a group of spiritual radicals or 'pneumatics' who, in reaction to the first group, exaggerated the concept of 'freedom'. This group was opposed to Paul's notion of the basic relationship between the Hebrew historical and moral tradition and the Christian faith. They disparaged Paul personally and charged him with holding a subordinate position in subjection to the Jerusalem apostles to whom they themselves held no allegiance. They also accused him of adapting his gospel to the needs of his environment, of having left his doctrine of freedom from the law, and of practically having preached circumcision itself. Thus while Paul's affirmation that justification comes by faith apart from the works of the law was directed against the judaizing group, his emphasis on the value of the Hebrew tradition plus many affirmations throughout the epistle were directed against the radical group.

In 1945 Frederic R. Crownfield rejected the Lütgert–Ropes position that Galatians was directed against two groups on the grounds that the epistle did not give the slightest indication of a two-fold opposition.[18] He proposed that the opponents were syncretists, who had possibly been members of a Jewish mystery cult, who sought union with deity in various ways, including circumcision. The resultant effect of their syncretism was 'the combination of some Jewish rites with laxity in morals'.[19] As to the interrelationship between the various parties, Crownfield suggested that Paul was allied with Jerusalem against the syncretists.

An explosive situation arose in Galatia when the syncretists came through and taught that a higher spiritual illumination could be reached through circumcision and possibly other rites and that Paul himself believed this but had avoided telling them of it because of his subservience to the conservative Jewish apostles. They further emphasized the divine nature of the law of Moses but held that its strict morality was dull and uninspiring. The Mosaic rites, they said, had meaning only as vehicles of hidden power. Paul, in his response to such syncretism, emphasized (1) his independence from the Jerusalem apostles, (2) the mutual exclusiveness of law and gospel, and (3) the moral imperative of Christian liberty.

In 1954 Johannes Munck[20] levied a broadside attack on Baur and the Tübingen school. Munck argued that the view that the gospel was for everyone including Gentiles was held by the Jewish church and Paul alike and that the difference between them was one of method not message. The Jewish church believed that the Gentiles would be converted when Israel came to faith; Paul believed that Israel would be converted when the Gentiles came to faith.[21]

According to Munck, Paul's opponents in Galatia were not Jewish judaizers but Gentile judaizers who had misunderstood Paul's teaching about Jerusalem and who were influenced by reading the Old Testament. Munck drew attention to the present participle, 'those who accept circumcision' (οἱ περιτεμνόμενοι), in Gal. 6: 13 and argued that it had to refer to those who were receiving circumcision, namely, Gentiles. Munck says:

> As the present participle in the middle voice of τεριτέμνω never means 'those who belong to the circumcision', but everywhere else 'those who receive circumcision', that must also be the case in Gal. 6: 13. That is made specially clear by the connexion between the two sentences. The thought here is not of the Jews or Judaizers in general, but specifically of the Judaizers among the Galatians. Paul's opponents who are agitating for Judaism among the Gentile Christian Galatians, are therefore themselves Gentile Christians. Their circumcision is still in the present, so that all this Judaizing movement is of recent date.[22]

In 1956 Walter Schmithals published an article entitled 'Die Häretiker in Galatien'[23] which he reissued in a revised version in *Paulus und die Gnostiker* in 1965[24] in which he argued against Lütgert and Ropes for a single battle line of opposition in Galatia. The opponents were Jewish or

Jewish Christian gnostics, who though they preached circumcision, had no connection with the Jerusalem apostles. Schmithals argued that the premise of the opponents, accepted also by Paul, was that 'purity of the gospel and the non-mediated character of the apostolate are inseparable'.[25] This gnostic belief was far from the position of the Jerusalem apostles. Furthermore, he argued that their non-connection with Jerusalem was clear in that they charged Paul with being dependent on the Jewish apostles. For them to make this charge while they themselves were dependent on the apostles would be to deny their own source of authority. He denied the argument that the opponents denounced Paul for not having lived up to the gospel as he received it from Jerusalem, an argument which, according to Schmithals, was merely a way out of an exegetical predicament, for to him 'the charge actually concerns dependence and not a single word concerns *apostasy*'.[26]

II

A common method used by all those who attempt to identify the opponents at Galatia is to analyze the charges against Paul and his responses to them. He is said to have been charged with being a non-genuine apostle, of dependence on man for his gospel, of apostasy, of time serving and changing his tone, of having dishonorably tried to please men, of abridging his message, and of preaching circumcision. Though some think the opponents were subtle in their approach, many believe that they openly brought hostile accusations against the apostle. Thus Baur says that the opponents used 'the most unjust accusations and the most malicious calumnies against the Apostle Paul'.[27] Ropes says the charges amounted to a 'personal attack upon Paul which he bitterly resents and to which he here replies in a good deal of heat'.[28] Schoeps says the opponents make an *ad hominem* attack on Paul.[29] Whether the charges were subtle or open most believe that the opponents can be identified by the implications of these charges against Paul.[30]

But an examination of the charges shows that there is no consensus of opinion as to what they actually imply. For example, one charge which most believe was made against Paul is that he is dependent on the Jerusalem apostles for his gospel. But this charge has received more than one interpretation. Ropes uses it to prove that the opponents in this case cannot have been Jewish Christian judaizers from Jerusalem for this would put the judaizers in a position of opposing Paul for being dependent on the Jerusalem apostles and drawing authority from them when that was the source of their own authority.[31] Similarly Schmithals argues that

> it is inconceivable that the Jerusalem apostles in Galatia accuse Paul
> of being dependent *upon themselves* or, in case they were only
> representatives of the Jerusalem authorities that *like themselves* he

is dependent upon the apostles in Jerusalem. Therewith one can indeed minimize his authority as an apostle, but certainly cannot reject his gospel.[32]

But on the basis of this charge others argue that the opponents are Jewish judaizers connected with Jerusalem. To them the charge is not simply that Paul is dependent on the Jerusalem apostles, but that being dependent on them he has not remained loyal to them. Thus Bligh says: 'The whole charge was that having received the gospel from the apostles in Jerusalem, he was not teaching what the apostles taught by diluting the gospel to please the Gentiles (cf. Gal. 1: 10).'[33] According to Bligh there is no implication whatever in this charge that the opponents are non-Jewish judaizers.

Another case where unanimity fails over the interpretation of a charge is the so-called charge of pleasing men implied from Gal. 1: 10. Ropes says that the charge is supplemented and probably explained by another charge implied in Gal. 5: 11 that Paul preached circumcision. In combination, the two mean that Paul is charged with preaching circumcision in order to please the Jerusalem apostles. Ropes says that this rules out the identification of the opponents as judaizers since

> this is a most extraordinary charge for judaizers to bring, whose own chief business at the moment was itself to 'preach circumcision'. We could understand such an allegation by them if they had claimed Paul as an ally, but Paul here evidently treats the statement as a hostile charge, to be repudiated with indignation.[34]

But completely to the contrary is the view of Munck. To him the charge is that Paul has sought to please the Galatians, not the Jerusalem apostles, by abridging the message which he got from Jerusalem.[35] This means that the opponents are judaizers though Munck claims that they are Gentile by race.[36]

From these examples it appears that the charge approach to the identification of the opponents causes diversity in interpretation. This is because the charges themselves are not clearly stated in the letter and come only as implications from some very brief and unclear statements. This leads us to question whether any direct charges were in fact made at all. As Jewett conjectured, it was not the strategy of the opponents to oppose Paul directly but to offer a completion to his gospel.[37] Thus it is possible that the opponents did not charge Paul outright but in a very clever way undermined his authority indirectly. Moreover, it is possible even to go further and argue that the opponents did not charge Paul at all, directly or indirectly, but actually considered him to teach circumcision as they themselves did and in fact treated him as an ally.

A close look at the so-called charges shows that there is good reason to argue for this last proposal because it is not really clear that actual charges were brought against Paul. Many of the statements which are supposed to have been made against Paul do not convey within themselves hostile notions, but can be understood as complimentary. Thus when it is said that Paul is dependent on the Jerusalem apostles, there is no indication that this is a disparagement of Paul's authority, as if to say dependence on the apostles is bad. Many no doubt considered it proper and honorable to be dependent upon them. Moreover, when it is said that Paul still preaches circumcision there is no indication that this is spoken in disapproval of Paul, especially since the opponents themselves preached circumcision. And when it is said that Paul pleases men, there is no indication that this is considered inherently bad. Paul himself recognizes the need for expedient action when it is done for the right cause and at times speaks in favor of it (Gal. 4: 18; 1 Cor. 9: 19–23). It is very possible that Paul denied these assertions, not because they in themselves were bad or that they were maliciously directed against him, but because in his mind (and perhaps in his mind only) they were damaging to his unique position in the church which was not fully known by the opponents. In his particular case only must it not be said that he is dependent on the apostles and preaches circumcision because he, as the apostle to the Gentiles, had received a direct revelation to preach a non-circumcision gospel. Thus while he rejects the affirmations of the agitators, there is no indication that the agitators themselves knew of his unique position in the church or that they directly or indirectly intended to undermine his authority. One can argue that the agitators not only preached a Jewish gospel but actually used the example of Paul to support their views.

Consequently, it is possible that a different approach to identifying the agitators should be made. The view presented here is that rather than assuming that the opponents held the opposite position from the one they ascribed to Paul, they held in fact the same position they ascribed to him and considered him as their ally. If this is true it is most likely that the agitators were Jewish Christian judaizers from Jerusalem[38] who preached circumcision and who said that Paul did the same because he like them was dependent on the Jerusalem apostles for his gospel.

It is noteworthy that this understanding of the opponents fits well with the details of the letter. The following scenario is a reconstruction of events, from this point of view, which led up to Paul's writing of Galatians.

First of all when Paul came to Galatia he came because of a weakness of the flesh (Gal. 4: 13) which was apparently a disease.[39] After he left, Jewish Christians passed through and were surprised to find the Galatians uncircumcised. When they explained to the Gentiles that their salvation would not be complete (Gal. 3: 3) until they accepted the law and had submitted to circumcision, the Galatians responded by explaining that Paul had said nothing about these matters. After the judaizers learned of the circumstances surrounding Paul's visit among them they surmised that Paul had held back his usual insistence on circumcision because of his illness. He was afraid that the Galatians would reject him personally (Gal. 4: 14) because of the disease and would not accept a circumcision gospel. Paul, consequently, had avoided mentioning circumcision at that time in order that he might first win their confidence (Gal. 1: 10); but he certainly intended to return later and complete the process. They assured the Galatians that this was the case since Paul, like them, had been commissioned by the Jerusalem apostles who likewise taught circumcision. There could be no doubt that a man of Paul's integrity and loyalty to the church taught circumcision (Gal. 5: 11). In fact his reputation with all the churches in Judea (Gal. 1: 22–24) made it inconceivable that Paul under normal conditions failed to teach the necessity of the law for salvation.

When Paul heard of the disturbance the judaizers had caused in Galatia by this reasoning he was pained (Gal. 4: 19). He had been led to believe from his Jerusalem meeting with the 'pillars' (Gal. 2: 1–10) that the matter of circumcision had been resolved as well as his conflict with judaizers and that he would have a free rein to preach the non-circumcision gospel to Gentiles. But now again here were Jerusalem teachers troubling (Gal. 1: 7) his converts over the matter of circumcision. And what was even worse, they were putting the words of their circumcision gospel into his mouth. In his letter he thus denies his dependence on the Jerusalem apostles and the assertion that he preaches circumcision. Whatever else the Galatians think they must not think that he preaches a circumcision gospel. Paul reaffirms what he had preached the first time by pronouncing anathema (Gal. 1: 8–9) on anyone, man or angel, who should preach anything other than precisely what he had preached in Galatia. Since the agitators had taken it upon themselves to speak for Paul, he emphasizes that the present letter is by him only, Paul in the flesh (Gal. 5: 2), and not by some would-be spokesman for him. At the conclusion he draws attention to his large writing (Gal. 6: 11), again emphasizing that he, Paul, and no one else is speaking.

As for the opponents' interpretation of his visit to Galatia, Paul could not have been more in disagreement. He did not dilute the gospel in order to please them and win their confidence. This did not correspond to the facts at all. His illness was not revolting to them (Gal. 4: 14); on the contrary, they received him as an angel of God, even as Christ Jesus himself (Gal. 4: 14). They would have plucked out their eyes and given them to him if it had been possible (Gal. 4: 15). This means that there was absolutely no compulsion whatever on his part to water down the gospel. They would have done anything he had asked including circumcision.

If this reconstruction of the events surrounding Paul's letter to the Galatians is correct, two conclusions emerge. First it is clear that there is no need to postulate an opposition of syncretists, radical spiritualists, gnostics, or any combination of them. The opponents were Jewish Christian judaizers connected with Jerusalem. Secondly, the opposition which appears in the letter is from the viewpoint of Paul. While Paul was hostile to the judaizers, there is no indication that they were hostile to him. Paul's hostility to them was caused by his earlier clashes with other judaizers who had sought to undermine his work. Paul had hoped that such clashes were over since the Jerusalem meeting with the 'pillar' apostles and his reprimand of Peter; hence his disappointment at the turn of events is understandable. But there is no reason to believe that the current judaizers were privy to these earlier clashes or to the agreements made at Jerusalem. The probability of this will be verified in Chapter 2.

For the present there remain three major objections to this theory which must be answered. These, in the order they are discussed, are: (1) the implications of the ethical section (Gal. 5: 13 – 6: 10), (2) the possibility that the opponents did not practise or teach the whole law, and (3) the participle, 'those who accept circumcision' (περιτεμνόμενοι), in Gal. 6: 13.

III

The implications of the ethical section

In the ethical section of the letter (Gal. 5: 13 – 6: 10) Paul argues that though the Christian has been called in freedom he should not use his freedom as an occasion for the flesh. In a similar way he contrasts walking by the Spirit and fulfilling the lusts of the flesh. With Paul the two are mutually exclusive. Such language makes it explicitly clear that Paul is concerned with ethical behavior in the Christian life. But what does this have to do with the situation in Galatia unless Paul is saying that the way of his opponents is the way to immorality? If this is the case, it is perfectly reasonable for Paul to attack them. If their way is so far removed from the Christian ethic that it results in immoral acts, it is incompatible with the Christian faith. But in this case can it be said that the opponents are Jewish Christian judaizers who are forcing the law on Gentile Christians? How can it be that nomists are accused of libertinism? As one writer recently said: 'A legalist cannot be an antinomian.'[40]

Those who believe that the opponents are Jewish Christian judaizers usually argue that Paul is not attacking his opponents at all in this section but is rather offering a defense to a charge directed against him that his gospel of freedom is antinomian. Baur explains the section as 'a warning against the abuse of freedom'.[41] Bligh says that Paul is warning 'that Christian freedom does not mean the end of all obligations; it does not mean that the flesh is released from all restraints and permitted to follow its own lusts'.[42]

There is some question, however, whether Paul offers a defense in this section. It is more natural to take his words as an attack on his opponents. Ropes argues: 'It sounds like a straightforward warning against lax tendencies addressed to persons who really needed it.'[43] Schmithals says that 'Paul himself in fact is making a charge, not defending himself'.[44] Jewett argues for a middle position, suggesting that the section, rather than being a defense of the Pauline gospel or an attack on judaizers, is a warning to the Galatian congregation itself which had accepted the nomistic teaching of the judaizers from Jerusalem, but for non-nomistic reasons. They had accepted circumcision and the cultic calendar because these corresponded to pagan notions in their religious background. Jewett says:

> It was their desire to gain the final level of perfection which led to circumcision when they heard from the agitators that such an act would *ensure* entrance into the mythical seed of Abraham. And it was their instinctive respect for the cosmic powers which led them to a celebration of the calendar whose mystery was revealed by the wisdom of the Old Testament.[45]

Thus while the Galatians accepted these nomistic rites they did not accept the ethic of Judaism but in fact believed that they had been set free from moral restrictions.

All of these interpretations share in common the avoidance of having Paul attack Jewish Christian judaizers. They say in essence that Paul either defends his gospel, attacks non-judaizing libertines, or warns the Galatians themselves about immoral conduct. That Paul attacks Jewish Christian judaizers on the basis of ethics seems out of the question. But, as we will see, there is very good reason to believe that in this section Paul does attack at least the theology of Jewish Christian judaizers on the basis of ethics.

First it must be noted that the conduct which Paul attacks is not the kind which rejects the standards of law for a totally unrestrained immorality. This is clear by the way he inserts disparaging references to the law within his ethical strictures. He says: 'If you are led by the Spirit you are not under the law' (Gal. 5: 18), or, 'Against such there is no law' (Gal. 5: 23). Twice he adds notes to the effect that law can be fulfilled without actually keeping the specific requirements of the law of Moses: 'For the whole law is fulfilled in one word, namely, love your neighbor as yourself' (Gal. 5: 14), and, 'Bear you one another's burdens and so fulfill the law of Christ' (Gal. 6: 2). These words seem to be spoken to those whose problem is their attempt to keep the specific requirements of the law. As an alternative Paul suggests that the spirit of the law is enough. It is therefore highly unlikely that these ethical remarks are made to antinomians. But this creates an apparent paradox of placing moral restrictions on nomists. The answer to this is that Paul's arguments are based on the theology of the opponents which in his view leads to immoral conduct. Paul's underlying thought is that which permeates his theology at its very core, namely, the law places one under sin. To attempt to keep the law ends in one's being sold under sin and doing the desires of the flesh.

This interpretation is supported by Paul's use of the word 'flesh' ($\sigma \acute{\alpha} \rho \xi$) throughout the letter. He uses it both in reference to immorality and to the law.[46] In Gal. 5 he argues that the flesh lusts against the Spirit and the Spirit against the flesh (vs. 17). The works of the flesh are the immoral acts of man including fornication, uncleanness, lasciviousness, etc. (vss. 19–21). The works of the Spirit are the good qualities of love, joy, peace, etc. (vss. 22–23). Those who belong to Christ have crucified the flesh with its passions ($\pi \alpha \vartheta \acute{\eta} \mu \alpha \sigma \iota \nu$) and lusts ($\dot{\epsilon} \pi \iota \vartheta \upsilon \mu \acute{\iota} \alpha \iota \varsigma$), (vs. 24). At the same time it is the law which is characterized by flesh. Paul queries whether the Galatians after having begun by the Spirit are now to be completed by the flesh (Gal. 3: 3). He says that those who force circumcision wish to make a show in the flesh and escape persecution (Gal. 6: 12). They wish the Galatians to be circumcised in order that they might boast in their flesh (Gal. 6: 13). In the allegory of the two women (Gal. 4: 21–31) Paul speaks to those who wish to be under the law. Those who are of the earthly Jerusalem have the slave woman Hagar as their mother and are themselves in slavery and belong to the flesh. Those who are of the heavenly Jerusalem have the free woman Sarah as their mother and are themselves free and belong to the promise. Just as it was before when the son according to the flesh persecuted Isaac, the son according to the Spirit, so it is now. Therefore, they should cast out the slave woman with her son in order that the son of the slave might not inherit with the son of the free woman.

These references make it clear that to be under the law is to live according to the flesh.[47] When Paul says: 'For freedom Christ freed us. Stand fast therefore and do not again be subject to a yoke of slavery' (Gal. 5: 1), he means that the Galatians, now that they are free, should not attempt to take on the yoke of the law. Likewise when he says: 'For you were called in freedom, brothers; only do not use this freedom as an occasion (ἀφορμήν) for the flesh' (Gal. 5: 13) he means that now that the Galatians are free they should not use their Christianity as a stepping stone into the law. This is why he immediately adds: 'For the whole law is fulfilled in one word, namely, love your neighbor as yourself' (Gal. 5: 14), the thought being, if it is the law you are worried about, the Christian principle of love has already fulfilled it in its entirety.

This language finds striking parallels in Romans. There Paul writes: 'For sin shall not reign over you, for you are not under the law but under grace' (Rom. 6: 14). Again he writes: 'For when we were in the flesh (σαρκί) the passions (τὰ πάθήματα) of sins which were through the law worked in our members in order to bear fruit to death. But now we have been released from the law, having died to that to which we were bound, so that we serve in newness of the Spirit and not in oldness of the letter' (Rom. 7: 5-6). He continues by saying: 'But sin, taking occasion (ἀφορμήν) through the commandment, wrought in me all kinds of lust (ἐπιθυμίαν); for apart from the law sin is dead' (vs. 8). The thought is clear: to be under the law is to walk according to the flesh and to be enslaved to the passions and desires of the flesh. To be free from the law is to be in the Spirit and to walk morally.[48]

We conclude that Paul's ethical section in Galatians is neither an attack on the libertinism of non-Jewish opponents nor a defense of his gospel in face of charges of libertinism. His thought is far removed from either of these. Rather his language suggests that the thrust of his argument is the theological claim that to be under the law is to be under sin. His words are directed specifically to a judaizing situation which would force the Galatians to complete their salvation by moving from the Spirit to the flesh. Far from presenting an obstacle to the view that the opponents are Jewish Christian judaizers, the ethical section supports it.

Did the opponents teach the whole law?

Another obstacle to the view that the opponents are Jewish Christian judaizers is their attitude toward the law. In Gal. 5: 3 Paul says: 'And again I bear witness to every man who accepts circumcision that he is a debtor to do the whole law.' Another reference appears in Gal. 6: 13 where the apostle says: 'For neither those who accept circumcision themselves keep the law.' It is strongly urged that these references prove that the agitators were not Jewish Christian judaizers for if they had been they would have taught the importance of keeping the whole law and would have kept it themselves. It is argued that Paul's language implies the opposite in both cases. Crownfield says: 'This would be impossible for real judaizers, but quite natural for the syncretists.'[49] Schmithals argues that if they had been judaizers Paul would not have had to remind the Galatians of the necessity of keeping the whole law. 'This the Galatians had apparently not been able to gather from the message proclaimed by the false teachers. No wonder, since Paul finds that those who were circumcised themselves νόμον οὐ φυλάσσουσιν [do not keep the law] (Gal. 6: 13).'[50]

Lightfoot, on the other hand, argues that the opponents were judaizers who were just insincere in their faith and practice.[51] Similarly, Bligh says that the judaizers circumcised the Gentiles without imposing on them the whole law because they simply wanted to return to Jerusalem to boast of their accomplishments.[52] Jewett, as we have seen, says that the judaizing program was simply an attempt by the churches in Judea to avert Zealot reprisals for consorting with lawless Gentiles. The church demanded only the most obvious requirements of the Gentiles, and out of a desire not to weaken their case, did not impose on them the whole law, which was in fact unnecessary for their purposes.[53]

However, there is reason to doubt that the letter implies that the judaizers taught only part of the law. In fact the statement: 'Those who receive circumcision do not themselves keep the law' (Gal. 6: 13), actually supports just the opposite of what it is said to prove. Far from implying that the judaizers taught only part of the law it implies that they taught all of the law (even though they may not have kept it as scrupulously as Paul's Pharasaic background would have demanded) for Paul attempts to undermine them by announcing the shocking news that they themselves do not keep the law. Unless the Galatians believed that their teachers kept it, it is hard to see what this passage means. But if the judaizers, after having taught the necessity of all the law, proved themselves to be law breakers, their influence would be damaged. It is this which Paul intends to show.

As to whether the judaizers were insincere in their law keeping, it is difficult to tell. But such an interpretation of their motives is unnecessary to explain their not keeping the law, for the notion of judaizers who do not keep the law is already clearly articulated in Paul's account of the Antioch incident. Paul rebukes Peter in the following words: 'If you being a Jew live like a Greek and not like a Jew, how can you compel the Gentiles to live like Jews' (Gal. 2: 14)? The point is that while Peter himself did not keep the law he compelled the Gentiles to keep it. The rest of the Jews were also involved in this hypocrisy, so that Peter was not alone in this action. In short, the letter itself presents ample evidence of judaizing Jewish Christians who did not themselves keep the law.[54] It may be that Paul's allusion in Gal. 6 is directed toward judaizers who, in a similar fashion to Cephas, attempted to compel uncircumcised Gentiles to accept the law while they themselves broke the law (at least according to their own standards) by associating with them.

An analysis of Gal. 5: 3 shows that Paul's purpose in this passage is not to call to the attention of the Galatians for the first time the fact that if they accept circumcision they are obligated to keep the whole law. Paul would have avoided doing this at all costs, for this might be construed to mean that the law would save if it were kept in its entirety. But we know for a fact that Paul believed that a Gentile would be lost if he even tried to be justified by the law (Gal. 5: 4). Nor are we to suppose that Paul tries to frighten the Galatians away from the law by saying 'the whole law' as if they would immediately recognize their inability to keep it in its entirety and thus abandon it. If the Galatians had suspected for one minute that Paul's complaint against them was that they were not keeping the whole law, it is likely that they would have responded with: 'All right then we will keep all of it.' Paul himself thought that the law could be kept for he affirms that he had done just that (Philip. 3: 6).

The meaning of Paul's language in Gal. 5: 3 is to be sought from a different point of view. The entirety of the context concerns freedom as opposed to slavery. Thus in Gal. 4: 1–11 he speaks of going back into the slavery of the weak and beggarly elemental spirits of the universe. In Gal. 4: 21–31 he allegorizes Sarah and Hagar in terms of freedom and slavery. He begins Gal. 5 with: 'For freedom Christ set us free. Stand fast, therefore, and do not again be subject to a yoke of slavery.' It is this context that governs Paul's thought in Gal. 5: 2–3. There he says that if one accepts circumcision Christ will be of no profit (οὐδὲν ὠφελήσει). On the contrary, if one is circumcised 'he is a debtor [ὀφειλέτης] to do the whole law'. The emphasis is on the word 'debtor' both in that it is the first word in its clause (ὀφειλέτης ἐστὶν ὅλον κτλ.) and that it forms a wordplay with 'profit' (ὠφελήσει) of the previous verse. Paul's point is not that one who accepts circumcision brings upon himself the added requirement of having to keep all the rest of the law, as if he were previously unaware of this. Rather it is that one who accepts circumcision *obligates* himself to the law. For Paul, to be a debtor is to be in bondage (cf. Rom. 8: 12, 15 – ὀφειλέται / δουλείας with Gal. 5: 1, 3 – δουλείας / ὀφειλέτης), and this brings upon man all the adverse effects of servitude such as slavery to the weak and beggarly elemental spirits of the universe. In short, it means separation from Christ and removal from grace. Paul's mention of the 'whole law' is probably a reference back to Gal. 3: 10[55] and in the present passage serves to emphasize the severity of the indebtedness.[56]

There is nothing in the letter to suggest that the opponents' attitude toward the law was unorthodox. In fact Paul's language supports the view that the agitators were Jewish Christian judaizers who taught the importance of the law for salvation.

The participle, οἱ περιτεμνόμενοι

A third obstacle to the view that the opponents are Jewish Christian judaizers is the participle, 'those who accept circumcision' (οἱ περιτεμνόμενοι) in Gal. 6: 13. Munck says: 'The Judaizing opponents in Galatians are Gentile Christians. That emerges from Gal. 6: 13, which reads, "For even those who receive circumcision do not themselves keep the law, but they desire to have you circumcised that they may glory in your flesh." ' [57] Munck's argument is that the present middle participle always refers to 'those who receive circumcision', never simply 'those who belong to the circumcision'; so it must refer to Gentiles. Others argue similarly. Charles Talbert says: 'The evidence of Gal. 6: 13 indicates that Paul's opponents were not even Jews, but rather Gentiles. At least the most natural reading of the present participle (οἱ περιτεμνόμενοι) points in this direction.' [58]

An immediate problem with this explanation is that it presses the contemporaneity of a verb which denotes a one time event. Thus Munck says: 'Their circumcision is still in the present, so that all this Judaizing movement is of recent date.' [59] But how can one's circumcision 'still be in the present' unless one is speaking of the very act itself? Are we to understand Paul to say that the ones who are being circumcised this very moment do not keep the law? Such an explanation is forced and trivial. Furthermore, Munck's own understanding of the present as referring to a movement of 'recent date' is an obvious relaxing of a strict interpretation of the present tense. To speak of a 'recent date' already is to include persons circumcised some time in the past. But to do this is to use the present participle adjectivally to refer to a class of persons characterized by performing an act. Many do take the participle as a kind of timeless present. Lightfoot translates: 'The advocates of circumcision'.[60] Bligh renders it: 'Those who go in for circumcision' or 'The circumcisers' and calls attention to John the Baptist who after his death was still called 'the one who baptizes' (ὁ βαπτίζων).[61]

Burton disagrees with this interpretation insisting that the participle itself must refer to the converts, not the judaizers (who are, however, the subject of the verbs in vs. 12, i.e. 'wish' (θέλουσιν) and 'compel' (ἀναγκάζουσιν)). He bases his reasoning on four arguments: (1) He doubts Paul could have alleged without qualification that the Jewish Christians did not keep the law. (2) If he had had the judaizers in mind he would not have written the superfluous participle since 'keep' (φυλάσσουσιν) in vs. 13 would have had the same subject as 'be persecuted' (διώκωνται) in vs. 12. (3) The tense of the participle is against it, for although a general present may refer to a class of persons characterized by having done the action denoted by the verb, such a force is employed only if 'the mind is directed to the performance of the action, as distinguished from the resultant fact'. Burton sees no motive for such a distinction here if Paul had had the judaizers (or Jews) in mind. For this he would have had to write 'have been circumcised' (περιτετμημένοι). Furthermore, elsewhere in the epistle the present participle, infinitive, or subjunctive of 'to circumcise' (περιτέμνειν), i.e. Gal. 5: 2, 3; 6: 12, 13b, means 'to receive circumcision/to get circumcised' not 'to be a circumcised person'. (4) Confirmation comes from Gal. 5: 3 which shows that the judaizers had not yet brought the Galatians under obedience to the whole law.[62]

The problem with this interpretation, a problem which Burton himself anticipates, is the grammatical harshness of having different subjects in vs. 13a and in vss. 12 and 13b. In other words Burton's explanation has the judaizers as the subject of 'wish' (θέλουσιν), 'compel' (ἀναγκάζουσιν), and 'be persecuted' (διώκωνται) in vs. 12, for 'wish' (θέλουσιν) and 'might boast' (καυχήσωνται) in vs. 13b, while it has the Galatians as the subject of 'those who accept circumcision' (οἱ περιτεμνόμενοι) and 'keep' (φυλάσσουσιν) in vs. 13a. He argues that all possible ambiguity about the subject of 'wish' (θέλουσιν) in vs. 13b vanishes 'by the close parallelism between θέλουσιν ὑμᾶς περιτέμνεσθαι ['they wish you to be circumcised'], v. 13b and ἀναγκάζουσιν ὑμᾶς περιτέμνεσθαι ['they compel you to be circumcised'] of v. 12'.[63]

Conversely, Jewett argues that the subject of 'those who accept circumcision' (οἱ περιτεμνόμενοι) of vs. 13a is the same as the subject of the verb in vs. 13b and therefore one should expect congruity in the two in regard to the circumcision. In order to provide this congruity he takes περιτεμνόμενοι as a middle with a causative force and translates: 'For even those who cause to be circumcised do not themselves keep the law, but they desire to have you circumcised that they may glory in your flesh.'[64] This also is congruous with vs. 12 which speaks of those 'who compel you to be circumcised'. Such a causative use of the middle may occur in Greek[65] though it is somewhat rare in the New Testament.[66] However, such an understanding of the participle does make sense in the context even though the rarity of the construction and the apparent meaning of the present middle/passive in Gal. 5: 2, 3 causes reservations.

In short, Gal. 6: 12–13 is ambiguous. It would appear either that (1) the subject of all the verbs in vss. 12 and 13 is the same and refers to the judaizers (Jewett, Lightfoot, Bligh, etc.) or (2) the subject of vss. 12 and 13b is the judaizers while that of vs. 13a is the Galatian converts (Burton). A third possibility, which seems least likely, is that the subject of all the verbs in vss. 12 and 13 is the Gentile judaizers (Munck).

We may end this chapter by summarizing our conclusions. The agitators at Galatia were Jewish Christian judaizers from Jerusalem who were forcing the Galatians to be circumcised and to keep the law. They did not themselves oppose Paul but insisted that he like them taught circumcision. The letter to the Galatians is Paul's response to them. Though he treated the judaizers with contempt, there is no evidence that they treated him with contempt. The section on ethics is not a defense of Paul's theology nor an attack on non-Jewish judaizers. Rather it is a theological attack on Jewish Christian judaizers based on the view that keeping the law leads to servitude to sin. Paul does not reveal for the first time that circumcision obligates the Gentiles to keep the whole law. His emphasis rather is on the concept of 'debtor'. To accept circumcision makes one a slave all over again. Finally, the present participle in Gal. 6: 13 does not prove that the agitators are Gentiles. The most likely interpretations of this statement fit into the explanation that the agitators are Jewish Christian judaizers from Jerusalem.

2

PAUL THE APOSTLE TO THE GENTILES

When we come to the autobiographical section of Galatians (1: 13 - 2:14) it is widely held that Paul's purpose is to prove, in face of charges to the contrary, that he is independent of the Jerusalem apostles and that they fully recognize his apostolic position in the church.[67] The letter begins: 'Paul an apostle, not from men nor through man but through Jesus Christ.' The point is held to be clear. 'Paul is said to have received his apostolate, not immediately from God, as befits an apostle, but from or through men.'[68] According to this theory, the apostle denies his dependency on the other apostles by describing his past relationship with them as being limited and for the most part amiable. At the time of his conversion he conferred with no one, not even the Jerusalem apostles. Only after a stay in Arabia and a lapse of three years did he go up to Jerusalem for the first time after his conversion. Even then he stayed only fifteen days with Peter and of the other apostles he saw only James. For the truth of this he calls God as a witness. Then he went into the regions of Syria and Cilicia and remained unknown personally to the Judean churches. They only heard that he was now preaching the faith that he once persecuted and they glorified God. Then after fourteen years[69] he went up to Jerusalem again, by revelation, and met with the apostles. At that meeting they gave to him and Barnabas the right hand of fellowship that he should go to the Gentiles and they to the Jews. Unfortunately, at a later date when Cephas came to Antioch, Paul was obliged to rebuke him to his face because he was not walking according to the truth of the gospel.

Since the time of Baur this section of the letter has been contrasted with the parallel account in Acts 9: 1ff. It is argued that in Galatians Paul seeks to establish his independence from the Jerusalem apostles by pointing to the length of time between his conversion and his first visit and the infrequency of later visits, viz., only one other in fourteen years. In Acts, on the other hand, Paul comes to Jerusalem not long after his conversion (Acts 9: 23 - 'many days') and frequently visits the Holy City thereafter. If Paul's fourteen-year visit in Galatians corresponds to the Jerusalem Council of

Acts 15, it is believed that Luke is either wrong about the intermediate famine visit of Acts 11 - 12 or that Paul grossly misrepresents the facts when he seeks to establish the infrequency of his Jerusalem visits.[70]

A look at the context of Galatians, however, shows that the traditional understanding of Paul's purpose in this section is problematic. Although it is clear that Paul was independent of the Jerusalem apostles, his method of presenting the events of his Christian career creates doubts as to whether his purpose in recording them was actually to prove his independence. In the following discussion we will point out some obstacles to the view that Paul uses this narrative to *prove* his apostolic independence. We will then reinterpret the entire section to show that Paul's point is quite different from the traditional view. Paul's account of the belatedness and the infrequency of his Jerusalem visits, in our view, was to inform the Galatians that he did not tell the Jerusalem apostles of the uniqueness of his apostolic call until his fourteen-year visit. During the first three years he told them absolutely nothing. On his three-year visit he met only with Cephas probably in order to acquire some important facts about the life of Christ. He did see James, but none of the other apostles. We will further argue that 'by revelation' in Gal. 2: 2 means that the fourteen-year visit was for the specific purpose of passing on to the 'pillar' apostles, for the first time, an account of Christ's revelation to him of the non-circumcision gospel. All of this, in our view, was designed to explain to the Galatians how judaizers, who were supposedly in agreement with the Jerusalem apostles and even Paul himself, could bring a report that circumcision was essential to salvation. The answer is that Paul had just recently disclosed to the 'pillar' apostles his non-circumcision gospel and that there had been insufficient time for this new development in the church's mission to have been understood by all and for the news of it to have been thoroughly and properly circulated.

I

The juxtaposition of Gal. 2: 1–10 and Gal. 2: 11–14 opposes the usual understanding of independence with recognition. It is argued that in Gal. 2: 1–10 the apostles in Jerusalem acknowledge Paul's apostleship and mission to the Gentiles and thereby agree with him on his independence. As Lightfoot says: 'Their recognition of his office is most complete. The language is decisive in two respects: it represents this recognition *first* as thoroughly mutual, and *second* as admitting a perfect equality and independent position.'[71] But then Paul recounts his clash with Peter at Antioch after this 'agreement' and the two appear to be in disagreement. If it is important for Paul's argument that the apostles are agreed on his independence, his account of the Antioch incident comes at a most inopportune moment.

It was this fact that led the way for Baur, in the last century, to argue that the position of the Jerusalem apostles was basically Jewish. According to him they agreed with Paul only as a concession and only when pressed by the younger apostle. That their minds were unsettled about the whole affair is shown by their passive attitude toward the Gentile mission after their acknowledgement of Paul. Moreover, at Antioch, when Peter was faced with the practical realities of life and the urging of James, his true feelings emerged.[72]

Munck clearly sees the problem of the Antioch episode and explains it on two grounds. First he argues that any explanation which suggests that Peter disagreed with Paul theologically goes counter to the gist of Paul's demonstration of independence. If Peter did not agree with Paul he could not have accepted his witness to the gospel as valid nor could he have acknowledged Paul as an independent apostle of equal rank with himself and the others. On the strength of the flow of the argument, then, he suggests that between the lines is an 'absolutely necessary assumption' that gives the point of the episode, 'namely, that Peter gave way and allowed that Paul was right'.[73] Second he argues that there is no assurance that the episode came after the agreement in Jerusalem. The account begins with the words: 'But when he came' ($\ddot{o}\tau\epsilon$ $\delta\grave{\epsilon}$ $\mathring{\eta}\lambda\vartheta\epsilon\nu$), Gal. 2:11, which resembles 'but when it pleased' ($\ddot{o}\tau\epsilon$ $\delta\grave{\epsilon}$ $\epsilon\mathring{v}\delta\acute{o}\kappa\eta\sigma\epsilon\nu$), Gal. 1:15, with which Paul began the account of his conversion and not like the reports of his successive visits to Jerusalem, which begin with 'then' ($\ddot{\epsilon}\pi\epsilon\iota\tau\alpha$), Gal. 1:18, 2:1. Therefore Munck thinks it is possible that the Antioch incident took place at some unspecified time before the Jerusalem meeting.[74] He argues that Paul places it after his report of the Jerusalem meeting not for chronological reasons but because it is the clearest proof of his independence.[75]

The problem with Munck's explanation is obvious. It is most unlikely that Paul would have silently passed over the conclusion of the event, to be inferred by a reading between the lines, when the conclusion was an 'absolutely necessary assumption' for the episode. Furthermore, Paul had just accused Peter of hypocrisy. To leave the conclusion unstated, if indeed the matter had already been resolved at the time of writing, would be to cast the readers into confusion over what to believe about the relationship between Peter and Paul, if not to convince them outright of their mutual hostility. In short, the more probable conclusion is either that (1) the matter had not been resolved at the time of writing,[76] or (2) the conclusion was unimportant to Paul's argument. Moreover, even though it is possible to argue that the Antioch incident took place before the Jerusalem meeting, it is highly unlikely that it did. If Paul had placed it after his account of the Jerusalem meeting, without any notice of its true chronological position, he would have created unnecessarily a severe obstacle to his argument.[77]

But most have tackled the problem in another way. The problem exists only if it can be shown that Paul attacks Peter theologically for a belief in circumcision and law-keeping as a *sine qua non* for salvation. Most argue that the accusation against Peter was not made in regard to his theology, but to his actions. Thus Hort says: 'It is astonishing that any one should ever have thought this passage evidence of antagonism in principle between the two Apostles ... What St Paul rebuked was not a doctrinal but a moral aberration of St Peter: he was simply unfaithful to his own convictions.'[78] Likewise Bruce says that Peter's actions were 'a temporary concession for the sake of peace, and perhaps also for the sake of avoiding offence to scrupulous brethren' and that Paul reckoned his actions as play-acting in that they 'did not reflect his personal convictions'.[79] Schoeps says: 'The regrettable incident in Antioch was merely episodic, occasioned by uncertainties about the correct procedure for mixed Christian communities.'[80]

According to Schmithals, Peter's mistake was eating with the Gentiles in the first place for this ran counter to the intention of the Jerusalem agreement. 'Table-fellowship with Gentile Christians was a first step on a road on which there was no stopping, and, in the eyes of the Jews standing outside, this step for uniting the groups in the community must have made it look as if Jewish Christianity had already abandoned the Law completely.'[81] Therefore when James sent word to Peter of the problems his actions were creating for the church in Jerusalem in face of Jewish opposition, he withdrew from table-fellowship with the Gentiles out of fear *of* the Jews and out of fear *for* the churches of Judea.[82] Thus it was not a theological issue at all with Peter but one of urgent practicality. Schmithals further argues that Paul does not charge Peter expressly with theological wrong but with hypocrisy; if it had been a matter of Peter's decision against justification by faith apart from the law he would have charged him not with hypocrisy but with lapsing into unbelief. The hypocrisy of Peter which caused Paul alarm was his inconsistent behavior. If Peter, like James, had remained separate from the Gentiles there would have been no problem; but for him to form an association with the Gentiles and then withdraw was a reprehensible act.[83]

From the point of view of these statements, Peter's actions, whether starting with the time of his eating with the Gentiles or with the time of his withdrawal, were culpable, but not his theology. If this is so, the incident, even though coming after the Jerusalem agreement, does not present a real obstacle to the usual understanding of Paul's argument of independence. His argument is that in Jerusalem the apostles recognized his independence and at Antioch, when Peter made a practical blunder, Paul's apostolic office allowed him to set Peter straight.

But it is just this understanding which we challenge for there are strong reasons to believe that not only were Peter's actions called into question but his theology as well. First of all it is noteworthy that although Paul accuses Peter of hypocritical action (viz., though he himself lived like a Greek he compelled Gentiles to live like Jews) he answers him with the theological premise of justification by faith apart from the works of the law. While it is unclear where Paul breaks off a reporting of his words to Peter and resumes his instructions to the Galatians, it is most likely that Gal. 2: 15–17, and perhaps 2: 18–21, record at least the essence of his rebuke to Peter. This rebuke, though not lacking in ethical implications, is foremost an argument from theology. It seems unlikely that Paul would have spoken in such a manner if only Peter's actions had been in question.

But there are even more telling reasons to suppose that Peter's actions involved theological issues. These may be summarized under four heads: (1) the verb 'to compel', (2) the role of Barnabas, (3) Peter's hypocrisy, and (4) the position of the audience.

(1) In his rebuke Paul accuses Peter of compelling (ἀναγκάζεις) Gentiles to live like Jews.[84] This makes it appear that Peter was attempting to proselyte Gentiles into acceptance of the law. To mitigate the literal force of this verb it has become popular to understand it as referring merely to the implications of Peter's actions which were ambiguous and open to misunderstanding. It is argued that Peter did not actually believe that circumcision was necessary for Gentiles to be saved, but out of the exigencies of the moment his actions made it appear that he did. Thus Lightfoot says that Peter's fault was that he 'should *practically force* [emphasis mine] the ritual law on the Gentiles'.[85] Hort says that Peter's actions meant that Gentiles 'were now to be *practically exhibited* [emphasis mine] as unfit company for the circumcised' and that Peter's behavior 'was *in effect* [emphasis mine] a summons to them to become Jews'.[86] Schmithals says that ἀναγκάζειν ιουδαΐζειν can only mean 'indirect compulsion'.[87] In basic agreement with this is Duncan who says that Peter's real attitude toward the matter was to 'let the Gentile–Christians keep *their* customs, while *we* keep *ours*'.[88]

An assumption which is necessary to the view that Peter's actions were open to interpretation is that Peter withdrew without clearly stating his reasons. And yet it is so inconceivable that the apostle would have done so that it must not be true. Are we to believe that Peter withdrew from his Gentile brethren as an expedient, perhaps only temporary, concession in regard to a practical problem in Jerusalem (whether regarding Jews, Jewish Christians, or both is immaterial) without explaining his actions to his brethren?[89] If James had sent word of problems which Peter's actions were causing, is it not likely that Peter would have explained his predicament and his necessity to withdraw? If Peter on this occasion was still in agreement with Paul that the Gentiles *must* not be circumcised, would he not have called the church together and explained that there was no need on their part to be alarmed or to think that they were second-class citizens, but that in fact they were all right, and that it was only out of the exigencies of the hour, due to persecution against the Judean churches (or whatever) that he had to separate himself from them? Would he not in fact have made a full explanation of the situation, with the result that the church would have understood it and that would have been the end of the matter?

In light of this overwhelming probability of what the apostle would have done in such a practical situation as we have assumed, are we not compelled to assume that such a practical situation did not exist at all? The fact that Paul rebuked him to his face before all and accused him of compelling Gentiles to live like Jews points strongly to the conclusion that, regardless of what Peter himself personally believed, he was compelling Gentiles to be circumcised and that this compulsion was not the mere implication of an ambiguous act that had received no official explanation. In short, Peter was teaching outright that Gentiles had to be circumcised to be saved.

(2) The role of Barnabas in the Antioch incident is instructive in that Barnabas, like Paul, was given at the Jerusalem meeting the apostles' right hands in fellowship to go to the Gentiles. He also knew that the intention of the 'pillars' was to confine themselves to the Jews. If then the need arose for Peter to withdraw from the Gentiles for practical reasons he, above any one else, with the possible exception of Paul, would have appreciated Peter's predicament. At the same time he could hardly have attached this need to himself since he had already been given the go-ahead by Jerusalem to be a missionary to the Gentiles with all that that involved, including especially table-fellowship, since without that no mission program could have existed at all. The withdrawal of Barnabas hardly could have been for any other reason than a new theological conviction, spawned by Peter, that the Gentiles must be circumcised to be saved. How could Barnabas, a missionary to the Gentiles, who had received the right hand of fellowship from Peter, James, and John, who had dedicated his life to the Gentile mission and had already spent many years in its service, withdraw from the Gentiles, turn his back on his own converts, and not offer any

explanation himself to clear up the matter and do so merely in regard to a practical situation in Jerusalem? It is inconceivable that Barnabas, without long and serious consultation with both Peter and Paul and without firm assurances from the former of the absolute necessity of his actions, could turn his face toward Jerusalem and leave his brethren behind. Even if anyone else could have been content to leave Peter's actions ambiguous and open to interpretation, Barnabas would have withdrawn only out of absolute theological conviction.

(3) It is often held that Paul's charge of hypocrisy against Peter is evidence that Peter did not in fact have a theological problem on this occasion. As Bruce says: 'If Paul at Antioch charged Peter with "play-acting"...it was precisely because Peter on this occasion was acting in a manner at variance with his real principles.' [90] Even more forceful is the argument of Schmithals:

> Whatever the precise meaning given to ὑποκρίνειν may be, it completely excludes the possibility that Peter made a breach with the Gentile–Christian church owing to a private decision against the doctrine of justification by faith. For in that case Paul would have had to reproach him not with dissimulation but with lapsing into unbelief, with giving up the Christian fellowship altogether. [91]

Hypocrisy is often used in reference to a person who pretends to believe or who does one thing while in actual fact he believes or does something else. In the present context, although this basic understanding of the word remains, its actual meaning is determined by the chronological sequence of events. Paul says: 'If you being a Jew live like a Greek and not like a Jew, how can you compel the Gentiles to live like Jews?' This statement points to the disparity in Peter's earlier actions when he lived like a Gentile and his later actions when he withdrew from the Gentiles and compelled them to be circumcised. In other words, Peter's hypocrisy was not that he avoided the Gentiles, although his convictions told him that this was wrong, but that he did one thing for a while and later changed and did the opposite. He did not preach what he practised nor practise what he preached. If this is the case it is unclear which position actually represented Peter's personal convictions, whether that of entering into fellowship with Gentiles or that of avoiding them, though it is hard to escape the conclusion that he was convinced on both occasions that he was right. At any rate Peter's hypocrisy does not point to his personal conviction that he was wrong at the time he withdrew from the Gentiles. If anything it points to the fact that he went along with Paul's gospel for a while and then rejected it. [92]

But there is perhaps an even more significant implication in Peter's hypocrisy when the Antioch incident is contrasted with the previous meeting of Paul, Barnabas, and the three 'pillars' in Jerusalem. The association of Peter with uncircumcised Gentiles appears to be the result of the Jerusalem meeting. Especially the way Paul records the two events implies this connection. Therefore, when Peter withdrew from the Gentiles there is not only the disparity between his former actions at Antioch and his later withdrawal, but also a disparity between the Jerusalem agreement, where Peter gave his consent to the non-circumcision gospel, and his later withdrawal.[93] In other words we must not overlook the possibility that the two events, recorded as they are side by side, show that Peter broke faith with his former agreement with Paul.

(4) We can learn much by projecting the point of view of the audience in this case. If we assume that the Antioch incident was episodal and pertained only to the practical matters of Jews associating with Gentiles and not to doctrinal differences between Peter and Paul we must further assume that the Galatians did not know the details of the event or otherwise they would not have had their particular problem of circumcision. If they had known all along that Peter and Paul agreed that the Gentiles were not to be circumcised while the Jews would continue to practise circumcision out of deference to their national and ethnic heritage, it is most unlikely that they would have ever seriously considered the necessity of circumcision. The overwhelming implication of the letter as a whole is that the Galatians did not know any of these distinctions between Jewish and Gentile practices, and that though they may have heard of a meeting between Paul and Peter they did not actually know the details. But if they did not know the distinction between Jewish and Gentile practices, that is, that Jewish Christians practised circumcision while Gentiles did not, nor the details of the Antioch confrontation, Paul was hopelessly confusing his readers by his account of the incident unless he intended to convey to them that Peter tried to force circumcision on the Gentiles and was wrong for doing it.

When Paul related how Peter withdrew from the fellowship of the Gentiles, compelled the Gentiles to be circumcised and did not walk uprightly in regard to the gospel, how else were the Galatians to understand this other than that Peter had broken faith with his earlier agreement and had gone back to the law? Are we to suppose that they read between the lines and understood that Peter had simply withdrawn to a more Jewish Christian stance which after all was quite different from that of the Gentiles and that all that Peter was guilty of was his not making himself clear and leaving his actions open to misunderstanding? They could have done this only if they had had a clear perception of the differences in Jewish Christianity, with its practice of the law, and Gentile Christianity, with its separation from the law. But it is clear from a reading of the letter that they had no understanding of this distinction at all. The reason they were accepting circumcision in the first place was because they had come to believe that it was necessary for salvation and this means that they had no accurate previous knowledge of the different roles Jews and Gentiles were to play in the church. When the Galatians read Chapter 2 of Paul's letter they must have concluded that Peter actually wavered during the Jerusalem meeting, and that his true feelings, which were in fact the same as those of the judaizers who had recently taught them the necessity of circumcision, came out later when he withdrew from the uncircumcised Gentiles.

If the above arguments are sound, it follows that Paul actually places considerable distance between himself and Peter by his account of the Antioch clash. If his purpose in this section is to show that the Jerusalem apostles recognized his apostolic office as equal with theirs, he does not avail himself of the most effective way of doing it. One could argue, from the flow of the context, that Peter and Paul were poles apart in their understanding of the gospel and this naturally implies that Peter's recognition of Paul and his gospel was something less than enthusiastic.

II

Paul's account of the fourteen-year visit (Gal. 2: 1–10) also presents obstacles to the usual understanding of Paul's argument of independence with apostolic recognition. It is usually held that by this account Paul attempts to *prove* that the Jerusalem apostles agreed with him on the non-circumcision gospel and that they fully recognized him as an independent apostle of Christ. In this way Paul supposedly disproves the charges of the opponents that he is subservient to the Jerusalem apostles.

An examination of these verses, however, makes it questionable whether this is Paul's intention. First of all, the way Paul says that Titus was not 'compelled' to be circumcised seems to imply at least an attempt to have him circumcised.[94] If this is the case it appears that the apostles relinquished their demand only after considerable persuasion. This implies that they did not, at the outset, hold the same position as Paul did in regard to the Gentiles and that they conceded the case of Titus only after hearing arguments in his favor. Furthermore, the fact that Paul used the word 'compelled' implies that they could have made circumcision compulsory if they had so desired. It is difficult to understand Paul's choice of words here if after all they could not have had their way if they had so wished. The implication is that Titus remained uncircumcised[95] not because the apostles lacked the authority to demand it, but, due to the special arguments presented by Paul, because they did not demand it.

Moreover, Paul says that those who were of repute 'added nothing' to him. It is hard to understand this choice of words unless the apostles had been empowered to add something to him if they had seen fit. Paul could have said that the apostles were 'unable to add anything', if he had wished to emphasize his equality with them. But for him to say that 'they did not add anything' fails to suggest the equality with recognition which he is supposed to be proving in face of charges to the contrary.

Again, at the conclusion of his account of the meeting, Paul's language raises questions. He says that when the apostles *saw* (ἰδόντες) that he was entrusted with the gospel of non-circumcision and *learned* (γνόντες) of the grace given to him they gave to him and Barnabas the right hand of fellowship. Though the word 'fellowship' (κοινωνίας) denotes a mutual participation in the agreement, the fact that the apostles gave *their* right hands, and this only after they learned of the facts in Paul's case, implies (1) that they did not recognize his apostolic mission to the Gentiles before the meeting in the same sense as after it, and (2) the recognition of leadership and the extension of fellowship was from the 'pillar' apostles to Paul, not from Paul to them. Thus Paul's participation in the agreement was mainly one of acceptance only since nothing in the text suggests that the agreement was reached by a democratic process.

The account as a whole casts serious doubt on the view that Paul's purpose in recording the Jerusalem meeting was to establish his recognized independence from the former apostles. Even if Paul considered himself totally independent of them and of equal rank, his language in describing the event militates against the view that his purpose was to prove this. His language is spoken from the point of view of the 'pillar' apostles who apparently held that they could compel Titus to be circumcised, could have added to Paul's gospel, and could have withheld the right hand of fellowship. Whether or not Paul would have submitted to their will if their decision had been against him is irrelevant (though on the basis of the Antioch clash with Peter it is hard to believe that he would have submitted);[96] but the fact that he records the meeting in the way he does suggests that his purpose was something other than to demonstrate his independence.

One view of the original purpose of the meeting is that Paul went up to Jerusalem to make 'sure' that he and the Jerusalem leaders were in agreement in regard to the fundamentals of the gospel, so that Paul's Gentile churches would be recognized by the mother church as true Christians and real members of Christ's body. If after Paul's missionary efforts his converts were rejected as Christians and denied the status of members of the church, his work would obviously be undermined. But such a situation need not arise if only Paul and the Jerusalem 'pillars' could agree on essentials.[97]

The difficulty with this explanation is that if such a purpose is to be inferred from Paul's account, the text must have created problems for the Galatians over and above the ones it was supposed to solve. What were the Galatians supposed to think? Were they to think that fourteen (seventeen) years after Paul's career began as the apostle to the Gentiles and already after one trip to Jerusalem, he still was unsure that the Jerusalem leaders were in agreement with him on the fundamentals of the gospel, that it was possible that his converts would not be recognized by them as genuine Christians and real members of the church, that they might be refused the name of Christian and denied the status of members of Christ's body? Moreover, as they read of the conclusion of the meeting that the apostles themselves failed to take any part in the Gentile mission except only insofar as to ask about receiving money from it, and as they read of the clash between Paul and Peter at Antioch without being given any indication as to its outcome, they must have had serious doubts about the relationship between Paul and the Jerusalem apostles.

Another interpretation is given by Schmithals.[98] According to him a key to the correct understanding of the Jerusalem meeting is in the statement that Paul went up 'by revelation' (Gal. 2: 2), that is, he went not in obedience to a summons from the apostles, but in obedience to a divine command.[99] This suggests that it had been assumed erroneously that Paul attended the meeting at the behest of the Jerusalem apostles and that this assumption could have appeared only if it was Jerusalem that needed the meeting, not Paul. Schmithals denies that the motive of Paul's visit is made clear by the text but he is certain that it was not to get his gospel sanctioned by the authorities. As he says: 'No one is likely to want the *independence* of his gospel to be *confirmed*.'[100] He argues that Paul went up to the Jerusalem apostles out of consideration of a need of the Jerusalem church and that this need is implied by the agreements reached. The Jerusalem church needed to make assurances to the Jewish authorities that the mission to the Gentiles would in no way involve an attempt on the part of the church to turn Jews at home or abroad away from the law. Thus, according to Schmithals, the agreement was that Paul and Barnabas would confine themselves with their non-circumcision gospel exclusively to Gentiles, and the Jerusalem church, under the missionary leadership of Peter who taught the circumcision gospel, would go to the Jews both in Palestine and in the Diaspora. Of course it was understood by the church that the law would be kept by Jewish Christians only for practical reasons, not as a condition of salvation.

Schmithals further conjectures, along with Cullmann,[101] Dinkler,[102] and Klein,[103] that Gal. 2: 7ff. quotes from an official record of the conference,[104] which, according to Schmithals, was made to serve as documentary evidence to the Jewish authorities who possibly had representatives at the conference itself. The agreement would assure the authorities of the loyalty of the Jewish church to the law and thus secure their freedom from persecution from the Jews. At the same time Paul, who was leaving the coastal areas of Antioch and Syria for the larger untouched area of the Gentile world, wished to make sure that a Jewish Christian mission would be carried out by the Jerusalem church alongside his Gentile Christian mission.

Schmithals emphasizes that this agreement really meant nothing radically new but corresponded to what had in practice been accepted all along. It had been known and approved by all from the beginning that Paul's mission was to the Gentiles, not to the Jews, and that the gospel he preached was one which rejected the law (Gal. 1: 23f.). Moreover, these issues had no doubt been discussed during Paul's first trip to Jerusalem (Gal. 1: 18f.) and were answered at that time. Schmithals thus concludes: 'The statement "Each of the two sides should carry on his work in accordance with the principles observed hitherto" is no doubt true for the agreement made at Jerusalem.'[105]

But there are problems with this explanation of the event. In the first place, there is reason to doubt that 'by revelation' implies that Paul went up to Jerusalem by divine order. Since this will be discussed later we will leave it for the moment. If it does not have this meaning, however, the argument that Paul attended the meeting out of concern for a Jerusalem need is unfounded. Moreover, the words: 'Lest I was running, or had run in vain' (Gal. 2: 2), strongly suggest that the need was Paul's.[106]

Secondly, the agreement, as the above argument envisions it, was made in order to secure officially an arrangement whereby Jews would remain separate from the Gentile mission so that their observance of the law would remain pure. Paul was anxious to have assurances made to him that a Jewish Christian mission would be carried on parallel with his Gentile mission because his regard for the safety of his Jerusalem brethren restricted him from going with his non-circumcision gospel to Jews. But is this not highly unlikely in view of the behavior of Barnabas at Antioch? When Peter withdrew from fellowshipping the Gentiles at Antioch Barnabas did the same. This means that the position of Peter in regard to the Gentiles was the standard which Barnabas followed. That he accepted the Jerusalem agreement, then, strongly implies that it did not envision a separation of Jews and Gentiles. In other words, if the intention of the Jerusalem agreement was to separate Jews from Gentiles so that the Jewish observance of the law would remain pure and the Jerusalem church would be free from persecution, it is most unlikely that Barnabas would have continued as a missionary to the Gentiles since he himself was a Jew.

This leads us to question another aspect of Schmithals' thesis. He argues that the Jerusalem church needed to make assurances to the Jewish authorities that they were loyal to the law. According to him the Jewish church would have appeared to have completely abandoned the law if it united with the Gentile mission in the matter of table-fellowship.[107] Thus at a meeting, where representatives of the Jewish authorities were possibly present, they made an agreement with Paul and Barnabas and gave to them the right hand of fellowship that they should go to the Gentiles while they themselves remained with the Jews. They only asked that Paul and Barnabas raise a collection among the Gentiles for the poor among them. Supposedly an official record was made of this meeting to serve as documentary evidence to the Jewish authorities and thus protect the church from persecution.

But how could such a meeting have protected the Jewish church from persecution? The fact that they gave their right hands in fellowship to Paul and Barnabas, and requested money to be collected from the Gentiles to be brought back to them, far from separating the two groups, actually sets up the Jerusalem church as the sanctioning body behind Paul and his Gentile mission and in a position to benefit from it financially. That these two groups, so closely woven together, would remain separate in their dealings with each other must have been highly suspect in the minds of the Jewish authorities.[108] Moreover, that they sanctioned Jews to carry out this program (viz., Paul, Barnabas, and no doubt their many Jewish co-workers) meant not only that they allowed Jews and Gentiles to associate together, a thing which must have been odious to the observers, but also that they considered the entirety of the mission to be Jewish in origin. If the purpose of the apostles had been to assure the Jewish authorities of their loyalty to the law, it would have been far better to demonstrate this by some other way than to portray to the Jewish world that they stood behind Paul and his Gentile mission in this official manner.

What were the Jewish observers who were supposedly at the meeting to think when the Jerusalem apostles sent out Paul and Barnabas to the Gentiles? Were they to think that Paul and Barnabas would preach to the Gentiles but not eat with them? Schmithals himself recognizes the problem of Jews eating with Gentiles when he says of Peter's actions:

Table-fellowship with Gentile Christians was a first step on a road on which there was no stopping, and, in the eyes of the Jews standing outside, this step for uniting the groups in the community must have made it look as if Jewish Christianity had already abandoned the Law completely.[109]

If this is right, it is inconceivable that the Jerusalem church would have arranged a meeting, for the sake of the Jewish authorities, in which they sanctioned Paul and his Jewish entourage to carry out a Gentile mission which would unite the missionaries with their Gentile converts, among other things, in table-fellowship, the surest sign of social acceptance in the ancient Near East. If Peter's association with Gentiles endangered the Jerusalem church with the Jewish authorities, how could a meeting where the Jerusalem church *officially* sanctioned such association, in the presence of the authorities themselves, assure their freedom from persecution?

In point of fact none of these steps demonstrates what this theory suggests, but on the contrary, they strongly imply that although the 'pillar' apostles themselves chose not to go to the Gentiles their actions brought the two groups closely together in that Paul's Gentile mission now had the official sanction of the Jerusalem church. Furthermore, the fact that the 'pillar' apostles made no effort to go to the Gentiles, but sent Paul and Barnabas out to them, suggests that the reason they did not go was something other than that they wished to keep Jews and Gentiles apart in order to please the Jewish authorities. A much more likely reason they did not go was because they understood from Paul's gospel a need to preserve a strong Jewish wing of the church which, though in full unity with the Gentile wing, even in the matter of table-fellowship, would retain its own particular ethnic distinctiveness.

It may be that Paul's silence toward the possible culpableness of James in the Antioch incident points to the fact that James understood Paul's gospel perfectly well and was in fact entirely innocent in the whole matter. Peter's actions at Antioch, however, show that although for the moment he accepted Paul's gospel, his mind was in an unsettled state and that this instability led him to turn back at what he interpreted to be a sign of trouble. What 'those from James' told him will never be known for sure, but it is conceivable that Peter's understanding of their message, and even the envoys' understanding of it, was not in complete harmony with James' intent. This point will be developed more fully later in this chapter and especially in Chapter 4 in a context which gives an important insight into the nature of Paul's gospel.

In view of the difficulties we meet in pursuing the theory that Paul's purpose in relating the account of his conversion and his subsequent visits to Jerusalem was to establish his independence from Jerusalem and the recognition of this by the apostles, it is necessary to review these verses again. We will attempt to show that Paul's purpose is quite different from the interpretations we have discussed.

III

Beginning with Gal. 1: 11–12 Paul sets the stage for his argumentation: 'But I make known to you, brothers, the gospel which was preached by me that it is not according to man, for I neither received it from man nor did I go through instruction, but it came through a revelation of Jesus Christ.' It is traditionally believed that Paul introduces a long argument for independence from the Jerusalem apostles by this statement. The idea is that he is independent of them, and in fact of all men, because his gospel was given by a direct revelation of Jesus Christ. This point obviously is valid to a certain extent. But it can hardly be Paul's purpose to argue this at this time since in the very next two verses he gives away the fact that he did receive something from other men, even before his conversion. In vss. 13–14 he describes himself as a persecutor of the church and this logically implies that he knew (at least in part) and opposed what the church taught. Moreover, elsewhere he admits having received information on the crucial events of the gospel, namely, the death, burial, and resurrection of Jesus Christ, and the fact of Christ's post-resurrection appearances to Peter, James, the Twelve, all the apostles, and to above five hundred brethren at once (1 Cor. 15: 1–7).[110] In view of this, it is hardly probable that Paul wishes to argue for the legitimacy and independence of his apostleship on the basis of having received absolutely nothing from men.

Paul's intention appears quite different from this if we take the *exact* wording of his statement. He says: 'The gospel preached *by me* (τὸ εὐαγγέλιον τὸ εὐαγγελισθὲν ὑπ᾽ ἐμοῦ) *is not according to man* (ὅτι οὐκ ἔστιν κατὰ ἄνθρωπον).' There are two inferences that emerge from this statement. (1) Paul is not saying that he received nothing at all about the gospel from any man, for that would place him in conflict with his subsequent statement about being a persecutor of the church. He rather means that *the particular form of the gospel preached by him* was not given to him by other men. As he proceeds, it becomes clear that the particular form of the gospel which he has in mind is that form which distinguished his preaching from all others, that is, the non-circumcision gospel to the Gentiles. As to the rest of the gospel which was shared in common by all apostles and evangelists Paul has no reference at all; it would have been virtually impossible for him to have learned nothing of these matters from other men, given his preconversion relationship with the church. (2) Moreover, while it appears at first that Paul is trying to prove the legitimacy and independence of his apostleship by this statement, the flow of the auto-biographical section as a whole shows that this is not the case. The context, as we will argue, strongly suggests that Paul's meaning is not that he is an apostle because he got his gospel directly from Christ, but that he got his gospel directly from Christ because no man had it beforehand to pass it on to him. When Paul says that his gospel 'is not according to man' and that he 'did not receive it from man' he is beginning a detailed account about the uniqueness of his gospel which is designed to explain the presence of judaizers at Galatia. The point is that Paul was the first one to receive this particular form of the gospel and his recent disclosure of it to the apostles had not yet 'trickled down' to the church at large.

This point becomes clearer as we proceed with Paul's next words.

> But when it pleased the one who separated me from my mother's
> womb and called me through his grace to reveal his son in me in
> order that I might evangelize him among the Gentiles, immediately
> I did not confer with flesh and blood, nor did I go up to Jerusalem
> to those who were apostles before me, but I went away into Arabia,
> and again I returned unto Damascus (Gal. 1: 15-17).

These words are usually understood as an argument to support the contention that Paul was independent of the Jerusalem apostles. When he denies that he conferred with flesh and blood or made contact with the other apostles it is supposed to mean that he had no opportunity to receive anything from men and consequently was independent of them. But from another point of view these words mean something entirely different. In our judgment, he means that at his conversion and for some time thereafter there was no opportunity for him to pass anything on to others. With these words Paul is saying that no one, not even the apostles, was privy to the terms of his commission which he received at his conversion, for at that time he revealed them to no one.

It has often been noted that Paul's call was different from the other apostles who were with Jesus during his earthly ministry. Paul, by contrast, was called to apostleship only after Christ's resurrection. But that which made his call different from the others actually lay in the commission he received, not in the time that he received it. His commission was to preach a non-circumcision gospel to the Gentiles. He was not commissioned to preach to the Gentiles simply because this aspect of the church's mission program was lagging or because God saw fit to appoint a zealous young man like Paul to make it more successful. Paul's call and commission was much more significant. When the apostle writes that God chose him from his mother's womb and called him through grace to reveal the divine Son in him in order that he might preach Christ among the Gentiles, he means that God chose him to preach a non-circumcision gospel to the Gentiles. To Paul this was a momentous event. It was the time when God took steps to expand his kingdom into universal dimensions by pushing its boundaries beyond the borders of the law. It was this commission to preach a non-circumcision gospel to Gentiles that was the unique element of Paul's gospel which no man had before his conversion.[111]

Next Paul says: 'Then after three years I went up to Jerusalem to visit Cephas, and I remained with him fifteen days. But other of the apostles I did not see except James the brother of the Lord.[112] Now that which I write to you, behold, before God I do not lie.' (Gal. 1: 18–20). It is usually assumed that Paul mentions his three-year visit in order further to prove his independence. Although the fact that the visit took place three years after his conversion once again underscores his independence from Jerusalem, it is in another direction that we are to find Paul's main line of argument. When he says that he did not go up until three years later, it is implied that the apostles had had no opportunity before this to hear from him an account of his revelation. Furthermore, Paul clearly implies that the purpose of his visit was only to visit Peter, not to make the revelation known.

Paul's choice of the word 'to visit' ($i\sigma\tau o\rho\tilde{\eta}\sigma a\iota$) is used only here in the New Testament and presents an interesting situation because it often means not simply 'to visit' but 'to inquire of'. Although Paul may have meant that he came only 'to visit' Peter,[113] the word he uses would not necessarily convey this to his readers. They could easily have understood from it that Paul came to learn something from Peter.[114] Therefore, if his purpose was to establish that he learned nothing from the apostles, his choice of words is unfortunate. But if his purpose was to show that his form of the gospel was received by revelation and that he did not pass it on to the other apostles at his conversion or even on his three-year visit,[115] it then makes no difference whether he went up merely 'to visit' Peter or 'to ask him questions'. What Paul wished to assert was not that Peter did not furnish him with information, but that he did not furnish Peter with information.

Moreover, if Paul had purposed on this occasion to pass on the terms of his revelation he would have made a point to see the church leaders as a group, but this he flatly denies. In fact he asserts, calling God as his witness, that the only other apostle he saw was James the Lord's brother. This solemn invocation to the witness of God has often been applied to Paul's argument that his visits to Jerusalem after his conversion were few and far between. The thought is that Paul establishes his independence from the apostles by showing that he did not see them for three years after he was called; and, as if to counter charges to the contrary,[116] he calls God as his witness that what he is saying is true.[117] In this connection it is noteworthy that God's witness is invoked after Paul's denial that he saw of the other apostles only James. If Paul had wished to establish the infrequency of his Jerusalem visits by this appeal to God's witness, it seems likely that he would have placed it at the end of Gal. 1 or better still after 2: 10. The position of his invocation suggests that what Paul calls God as a witness to is not that it was only after three years that he went up to Jerusalem but that on that occasion he saw of the apostles only Peter and James. This precludes any opportunity for Paul to have discussed his revelation with the apostles as a group[118] and suggests that this was not his intention in the first place. The implication is that even at this time Paul did not tell them.

He concludes Gal. 1 by describing the events immediately after his three-year visit to Jerusalem. He went into the regions of Syria and Cilicia and remained personally unknown to the Judean churches. In fact the only thing they knew about him was that the one who used to persecute them was now preaching the faith; and this caused them to glorify God. Often this account is taken to prove that Paul and the Judean churches were unified in their understanding of the gospel at a very early time. Any argument which suggests that the two were at odds over the role of the law is considered out of place since it is doubted that the Judean churches would have glorified God over a man who preached heresy. But to use this line of reasoning is to miss the point of the paragraph. Paul, rather than showing that he and the Judean churches had always been agreed on the law, is explaining why a confusion over the law could arise at this late date and why a situation could exist where Paul could occupy a place opposite to that of the Jerusalem apostles and the Judean churches. The explanation is that neither the Jerusalem apostles nor the churches in Judea were told of his special revelation at the time of his conversion or during his three-year visit. The Judean churches had only the vaguest knowledge about him at all. They only knew that he was now a Christian and was preaching the gospel.

The fourteen-year visit, which Paul describes next, now takes on new and significant meaning, for unlike the former trip which was made for the purpose of visiting (or interviewing) Peter, this trip was made in order to pass on the revelation to the apostolic authorities. Paul consequently takes Barnabas with him, his companion in the non-circumcision gospel, and Titus who becomes a test case of an uncircumcised Gentile Christian. He

specifically states that this trip was 'according to revelation' (κατὰ
ἀποκάλυψιν). It is widely held that by this assertion Paul means that he
went up to Jerusalem under direct orders from God. Supposedly this was
to dispel the assumption that he went up to Jerusalem on orders from the
apostles.[119] In this way he continues with his argument for apostolic
independence.

But there are good reasons to suggest that what Paul means is not this
at all, but rather that he went up 'on account of'[120] his initial revelation
of Jesus Christ. The reasons are the following: (1) Paul does not use the
word 'revelation' (ἀποκάλυψις) to mean 'oracle' in the sense of χρηματισμός
(Rom. 11: 4) or χρησμός, such as would be involved in a command (whether received directly or perceived spiritually) as 'Paul, you are to go up to
Jerusalem'.[121] 'Revelation' is used by him in reference to the great revelations of God's acts in history especially as they pertain to the fundamentals
of the gospel of Christ.[122] Thus he uses it in reference to the coming of
Christ (1 Cor. 1: 7; 2 Thess. 1: 7), the righteous judgment of God (Rom. 2:
5), the mystery that had been kept secret for eternal ages (Rom. 16: 25).
Even in 1 Cor. 14: 6, 26, where Paul envisions other individuals receiving
revelations, these are not oracular commands for them to go somewhere
or to do something, but are revelations pertaining to the interpretation of
the gospel. Thus they are to be done strictly for edification (οἰκοδομήν;
1 Cor. 14: 26). (2) The construction 'according to revelation' (κατὰ
ἀποκάλυψιν) appears only three times in the Pauline corpus, i.e., Rom. 16:
25, Eph. 3: 3, and Gal. 2: 2. In Eph. 3: 3ff. the writer says that the mystery
of the inclusion of the Gentiles was made known to him 'according to revelation' (κατὰ ἀποκάλυψιν). In the doxology of Rom. 16: 25ff. Paul expresses
glory 'to him who is able to strengthen you according to my gospel and the
preaching of Jesus Christ, according to the revelation (κατὰ ἀποκάλυψιν)
of the mystery which was kept secret for long ages but is now disclosed and
through the prophetic writings is made known to all nations'. In both in-
stances the revelation pertains to the inclusion of the Gentiles and probably
refers to the one received initially by Paul. (3) In Gal. 2: 2 the words
immediately following 'according to revelation' are explanatory of it: 'And
I went up according to revelation and I laid before them the gospel which
I was preaching among the Gentiles.'[123] The fact that Paul laid before
them the gospel he had been preaching strongly suggests that until this time
they had not actually heard from him about the uniqueness of his gospel.
It seems most unlikely that Paul would have made a special trip to lay out
before the apostles the details of a gospel which they already knew.

If our analysis is correct, then, Paul, in saying that he went up 'according to revelation', means that now at long last he is going up to lay before

the Jerusalem apostles the details of his conversion, that he was called as a
special messenger to preach a non-circumcision gospel to the Gentiles,
which he had in fact been preaching now for fourteen (seventeen) years.
Until that moment they had never heard from his lips a detailed account
of this revelation which he received at his call.

Furthermore, he explains his need to tell those who were of repute[124]
of the revelation at this time: 'Lest in any way I was running or had run in
vain.' Though we can only conjecture why Paul delayed in declaring his
revelation to the apostles, it seems probable that he wished to present it
to them only after his apostolic position and his Gentile mission had grown
strong enough to convince them of his divine approval. After all it would
hardly have done for him to have marched back into Jerusalem, after having
gone to Damascus to persecute the church, and to have announced that he
had just changed his mind about Christ and had in fact just been commissioned as *the* apostle to the Gentiles to preach to them a non-circumcision
gospel. Such action would have aroused immediate suspicion of fraud if
not outright trickery designed to catch the Jerusalem church off guard.
Moreover, it is possible that Paul's first Gentile converts were from those
who had earlier been proselytes to Judaism. 'In that case', as one interpreter put it, 'they could be regarded even after their conversion to faith
in Christ as guests and dependents of the Jewish Christian congregation,
and not as in any way endangering the position of the letter.'[125] As
Paul expanded his Gentile mission there would have been little occasion
for the apostles to have suspected a difference in his gospel after he failed
to explain it to them on his three-year visit and also because of the difficulties in communication in the ancient world.[126]

But the need had now arisen for Paul to lay his cards on the table since
judaizers were threatening to undermine his work. The syntax of Gal. 2:
4-5 is extremely problematic,[127] but it seems most likely that Paul alludes
to a situation in his churches where judaizers were trying to subjugate his
Gentile converts to the law. It is no surprise that judaizers should arise. If
Paul had never related his revelation to the Jerusalem authorities or to the
churches in Judea it was only a matter of time before a crisis would come,
when Jewish Christians in good standing with the apostles would meet
Paul's uncircumcised converts and attempt to bring them under the law.
In all good conscience they could report that the Jerusalem apostles had
always taught and practised a circumcision gospel and that even Paul himself, so far as they knew, who was in good standing with the apostles and
all the churches in Judea, preached circumcision as well (cf. Gal. 5: 11).[128]
It was at this time, due to these circumstances, that Paul made his fourteen-
year visit. The apostles must be informed so that Paul's gospel to the Gen-

tiles could be freed from the menace of Jewish Christians, who by the authority of the apostles themselves, were preaching the circumcision gospel to Gentiles.

According to Paul's description of the meeting it was a success. Titus was not compelled to be circumcised, though he most surely would have been if Paul had not first informed the apostles of his revelation. On the contrary, when they 'saw' that he had been intrusted with the gospel of the non-circumcision and when they 'learned' of the grace given to him, the 'pillar' apostles gave to him and Barnabas their right hands in fellowship. Who were they to withstand the will of God? When they were informed of Paul's special revelation they conceded that a non-circumcision gospel to the Gentiles was by divine authority and they gave their sanction to it. Moreover they arranged with Paul that he and Barnabas should go to the Gentiles and they should go to the Jews.

Often this is interpreted merely as a practical matter. There must be some definable leadership in the mission programs of the church so what could be more effective than that Peter should direct his efforts toward the Jews and Paul toward the Gentiles? As we have seen, it has even been suggested that there was a restrictive note in the decision, that Peter and the apostles with him would go to the Jews *only* and Paul and Barnabas to the Gentiles *only*. But this is totally foreign to the spirit of Paul's account. It was not that the apostles said: 'All right Paul, you preach the non-circumcision gospel to the Gentiles, but stay away from the Jews, that's our territory.' The language rather suggests that they said: 'Right, Paul, you go to the Gentiles with the non-circumcision gospel and we will go to the Jews with the circumcision gospel.' This is not to be taken as a religio-political restriction on either side. It rather reflects a theological implication inherent in Paul's gospel that the unity which was destined for the church was one which envisioned a continued ethnic and cultural distinction between the Jewish and Gentile wings of the church.[129]

The likelihood of this is seen clearly when it is noted that what the apostles acknowledged on this occasion was not just the Gentile mission, for that had been going on for years, no doubt with both their approval and participation. Nor was it that they acknowledged that Paul had become the most effective worker in the Gentile mission and should therefore receive apostolic sanction as the leader. What they acknowledged on this occasion was something they had not known before; they acknowledged the gospel which Paul had been preaching and which he, on this occasion, laid before them for the first time, namely, the non-circumcision gospel to the Gentiles. This acknowledgement was in essence a recognition of the need for a distinctive Gentile element within the church. Their mission to the Jews, in accordance with this recognition, was important for the other side of the coin. Its intent was for the purpose of preserving the distinctiveness of the Jewish wing of the church which was necessary to Paul's particular concept of Christian unity. Judging from Paul's discussion in Romans 11, the distinctiveness of each of these groups was important for the salvation of the other.[130]

In choosing to remain with the Jews the apostles in no way stepped down as 'pillars' of the universal church. The Gentile mission was as much an object of their concern as always. Therefore they granted to Paul and Barnabas the right hand of fellowship and they asked that they bring financial support for the poor from the Gentile Christians. There was no hostility or divisiveness in their attitude. Rather they showed full recognition of the importance of unity and took positive steps to secure it.

The Antioch incident now also takes on new significance. Paul and Barnabas were working together with both Jewish and Gentile Christians, who were practising mutual fellowship, including table-fellowship. Such a union under the sanction of both Paul and Barnabas makes it abundantly clear that nothing said at the Jerusalem meeting prohibited or in any way limited such fellowship. Moreover, when Peter came to Antioch he too entered into the mixed fellowship with the rest of the Jews and ate with the Gentiles. To do this must have meant a relaxing of the Jewish custom of not eating with Gentiles. The text makes it clear, however, that these actions were not in themselves so extensive as to hide the identity of the Jewish members of the church. It was clear to all who were the Jewish and who were the Gentile Christians.

But then certain ones[131] came from James, and Peter gradually ($\upsilon\pi\acute{\epsilon}\sigma\tau\epsilon\lambda\lambda\epsilon\nu/\grave{\alpha}\phi\acute{\omega}\rho\iota\zeta\epsilon\nu$) withdrew from the Gentile fellowship out of fear of the circumcision ($\tau\acute{o}\upsilon\varsigma$ $\grave{\epsilon}\kappa$ $\pi\epsilon\rho\iota\tau o\mu\widetilde{\eta}\varsigma$; Gal. 2: 12). It has been argued that the 'circumcision' can only refer to the Jews and not to the Jewish Christians,[132] and that Peter withdrew out of fear for the Jerusalem church which was receiving opposition from the Jews. This is most unlikely since it requires Paul to distinguish nominally between Christians and Jews. But Paul shows no tendency to do this in general. He had no qualms in considering himself in the basic Jewish categories (Rom. 11: 1; 2 Cor. 11: 22; Philip. 3: 3, 5). Furthermore, in the very next verse he uses the word 'Jews' ('$Iο\upsilon\delta\alpha\widetilde{\iota}o\iota$) to mean 'Jewish Christians'. Also at least once he uses 'circumcision' ($\pi\epsilon\rho\iota\tauο\mu\acute{\eta}$) to mean (Jewish?) Christians (Philip. 3: 3).

It is also urged by some that Peter simply made a practical blunder and that Paul's charge of hypocrisy actually implies that he was not behaving according to his own convictions. This explanation is made in order to refute the theory that Peter and Paul displayed theological differences on this occasion. But such a theory places the apostle Peter in such an ill-conceived light that one can only wonder about his moral character. Was Peter such a scoundrel that he preached a Jewish gospel to the Gentiles and all the while was fully convinced that they would be damned if they accepted it?[133] And did Barnabas go over to Peter on this occasion knowing all the while that the Gentiles would be lost if they practised circumcision and not offer any explanation for his actions that would salvage the situation? What kind of men were they to damn the souls of others simply for expediencies?

Does not the whole context suggest that Peter's behavior was conditioned by the abruptness of Paul's recent disclosure of the non-circumcision gospel which left him, perhaps unconsciously, unsure of what the relationship between Jewish and Gentile Christians should be? His first action upon arriving at Antioch was to Hellenize ($\dot{\epsilon}\vartheta\nu\iota\kappa\hat{\omega}\varsigma\ldots\zeta\hat{\eta}\varsigma$; Gal. 2: 14). Then certain ones came from James and he went to the opposite extreme; he withdrew from the Gentile fellowship and began to compel the Gentiles to Judaize ($\tau\dot{\alpha}\ \ddot{\epsilon}\vartheta\nu\eta\ \dot{\alpha}\nu\alpha\gamma\kappa\dot{\alpha}\zeta\epsilon\iota\varsigma\ ᾽\text{Io}\upsilon\delta\alpha\ddot{\iota}\zeta\epsilon\iota\nu$; Gal. 2: 14).

Paul's language in this section of the letter is most curious. His statements about 'certain ones from James' and his failure to include James in his public indictment reveals a caution on his part which should not be overlooked. First of all it may be that Paul did not want to indict James without first having faced him personally in order to see if Peter's reaction to the envoys was warranted. This suggests that Paul and James had had a full and mutual understanding at the Jerusalem meeting which Paul did not wish to question without hearing from James himself. Secondly, it may be that Paul suspected that Peter's reaction to the envoys was due to a misunderstanding of what James meant. Paul's brief description of the Jerusalem meeting and of the Antioch crisis leaves us with little information, but it could have been that Peter's acceptance of Paul's gospel at Jerusalem was of such a nature that even then Paul suspected that the understanding of James and John was better than that of Peter.

It is also possible that the message which James sent to Peter was a word of caution for him not to Hellenize completely, since this would lead to the eradication of the ethnic and cultural distinctiveness of Israel and its role in the salvation of mankind. If Peter's understanding of Paul's gospel was already unstable, as we have suggested as a possibility, it is not surprising to see in Peter's withdrawal from the Gentiles a misunderstanding of James as well. Moreover, the envoys themselves may have presented the message to Peter incorrectly due to their own bias or perhaps misunderstanding of the issue. At any rate, when Peter withdrew and took Barnabas and the rest of the Jews with him, Paul rebuked him publicly without a single reference to James. This means that the innocence of James and his full understanding of Paul's gospel as it was revealed at Jerusalem is not beyond the range of probability. Moreover, it strongly suggests that Peter's problem was his lack of theological understanding.

It is notable that Paul's charge against Peter was that though Peter had himself lived like a Gentile (just how far he went in his Hellenization Paul does not say, but certainly far enough for Paul to make a public issue out of it), he had now withdrawn and was compelling Gentiles to live like Jews. This means that Peter's hypocrisy was not a simultaneous action of doing one thing while being convinced that it was wrong, but rather of doing one thing for a while and later doing the opposite. When Paul telescoped these two together for the sake of making a public charge, Peter's guilt was said to be hypocrisy. And though from one point of view Peter's sin was hypocrisy, in that he did not practise what he preached, it must not be understood in the sense that Peter was convinced that he was wrong when he withdrew from the Gentiles. In fact the whole account implies that Peter withdrew from the Gentiles out of the frightful suspicion that what he was doing was not right, and that Barnabas went with him because Peter had convinced him that association with uncircumcised Gentiles was wrong.

Moreover, this serious questioning in Peter, stimulated by the envoys from James, was in all probability the natural result of the Jerusalem meeting when after many years to the contrary Peter was told of Paul's non-circumcision gospel. The surprising thing is not that he wavered in his understanding of the Christian faith on this occasion but that such waverings were apparently confined to this general time-period and in fact amounted to so little. We hear of no other such crisis in the church, and from all appearances Paul's one public rebuke of Peter was enough eventually to bring him around.

Paul's approach to Peter on this occasion confirms that the whole affair was a matter of Peter's understanding. Paul lectures to him about the implications of justification by faith apart from the works of the law. He says that they who by nature are Jews and not 'sinners of the Gentiles' (ἐξ ἐθνῶν ἁμαρτωλοί) know that justification is by faith apart from the works of the law. But if while seeking to be justified in Christ they themselves are found to be 'sinners' (ἁμαρτωλοί), i.e., eating with Gentiles,[134] this does not mean that Christ is a minister of sin. The meaning is that if a Jew seeks to be justified by faith and finds himself associating with Gentiles as a result, this is not something to cause alarm. Christ is not a minister of sin; so the mixed association has divine sanction.[135] Paul continues by saying that if the Jewish Christian builds up what he has torn down, that is, if he goes back to his Jewish way and breaks off with the Gentile fellow-ship, he constitutes himself (ἐμαυτόν) as a transgressor. This in fact is what Peter had done. So Paul's answer implies that in Peter's mind there was a serious doubt about his association with uncircumcised Gentiles; in fact he was fearful that it might have constituted him a sinner. Paul assures him of the divine sanctity of such fellowship and warns him that it is rather the breaking off of the fellowship or the building up of the barrier that he once tore down that will condemn him.

If we have interpreted these events in Paul's life correctly, it now remains to explain why he reports them to the Galatians. It is clear from the letter as a whole that the question with which they were faced is similar to that with which the apostles at Jerusalem and Peter at Antioch were faced. The question is: must the Gentiles keep the law? Judaizers had come to Galatia telling Paul's converts that among other things they must be circumcised. They reported that this was the gospel which the apostles at Jerusalem preached and, insofar as they knew, which Paul himself preached. That they were using subtle tactics to undermine Paul when they said that he preached circumcision (Gal. 5: 11), as some have suggested, is uncertain. It is highly possible that at the time these judaizers came to Galatia they actually believed that Paul like them preached circumcision. It no doubt took time after the initial disclosure of the revelation for the apostles to inform the church of the new developments in the Gentile mission.[136]

Furthermore, it seems likely that the Galatians themselves had little or no knowledge of Paul's revelation. In fact Paul's purpose in relating the details of his conversion and his trips to Jerusalem was to inform them. The major problem with the Galatians was their failure to understand the current situation in the church. Judaizers come saying that Paul and the apostles preach circumcision and that they are unsaved, an idea so far from their minds that they are totally confused. Maybe Paul did not tell them everything because of the particular circumstances of his entrance among them;[137] maybe the apostles do teach circumcision; maybe they are not saved! Paul's purpose then was to give a full airing to the whole affair. The apostles have taught circumcision and until recently had no reason to do differently. But all of this must now change in light of his revelation. What he preached to them before was not an abbreviated version of the truth; it was a straightforward proclamation of the gospel which Jesus Christ himself revealed.

So Paul's account of these events is not simply a *proof* of his independence from the apostles, but rather an explanation of the current situation.[138] It is in fact a powerful apostolic demonstration[139] by which Paul discloses the facts in the case and clears the air. When the Galatians learn of his delay in relating to the apostles the details of his revelation they come to understand how there can be a report that the apostles, including Paul, preach circumcision, when in fact they know by experience that Paul does not. This explanation removes their doubts and shows them that they are pioneers on the frontier of a new expansion of the church in which uncircumcised Gentiles are included into the church.

The implications of this explanation of the autobiographical section of Galatians, insofar as the history of interpretation is concerned, are far-reaching. It is not that judaizers supported by the Jerusalem leaders have been dogging Paul's steps all over the Mediterranean world in an effort to undermine his work. Even less is it that early Christianity represents a continual struggle between Peter and Paul. What we get in Galatians is a glimpse into that moment of Christian history when steps were taken to expand the borders of the church for the incorporation of all nations. Unlike before, when Gentiles were admitted on the basis of Judaism, Paul's mission was to place the gospel forever out of the realm of Jewish nationalism. From the moment of his revelation the church was destined to break the bounds of the law. But Paul necessarily had to face a critical moment when the truth of a universal gospel would be challenged. Not that the church would reject it and maliciously attempt to destroy it (though there were always some who remained obstinate),[140] but that such a world view of the gospel would create confusion and doubt in the minds of honest believers steeped in the ways of Judaism. How could men who had all their lives dedicated themselves to God's law break away from that law in their evangelistic efforts to Gentiles without suffering the pangs of death itself? How could Peter after hearing only once of the universal gospel from Paul not doubt and have fear for his religious safety when, in his mind, James was having reservations? This was no flaw in his moral character, as if he were repeating his denial of Christ.[141] It was not that Peter withdrew from the Gentiles knowing full well that he was doing wrong when he did it. He did what he had to do. He had to turn back until the matter was cleared in his mind and his doubts were removed. This Paul attempted to do when he explained to him more fully the implications of the gospel of justification by faith apart from the works of the law.

Though Peter wavered on this occasion, subsequent history shows that the matter was soon resolved.[142] When Paul writes 1 Corinthians it is with respect that he speaks of Peter. Nor is there any indication in all of the New Testament that a feud between the two was perpetual. From all appearances, the apostle, shaken as he was at the full disclosure of the gospel of Christ, soon incorporated it into his own preaching and allowed himself to become a foundation for unity in the church.

3

JUSTIFICATION BY FAITH

I

In the middle section of Galatians (basically Chapters 3 and 4) Paul's discussion is much more theological than that of Chapters 1 and 2. This is not to say that theology is altogether absent in the first chapters or that theology is everywhere present in the middle chapters. Rather it is to say that Chapters 1 and 2 are predominantly narrative and autobiographical; Chapters 3 and 4 are predominantly theological.

We must not assume that these chapters differ in subject matter simply because they differ in approach. Since the letter is relatively short, it does not seem unreasonable to assume that it deals with one major theme, and this all the more so, since the writer leaves behind no hints that he changes themes. It is likely, in our view, that the middle section of the letter, which discusses Paul's doctrine of justification by faith, relates directly to the theme of the inclusion of uncircumcised Gentiles into the kingdom of God, because this theme is a major motif of the first section of the letter. We will proceed by showing that most interpreters (Schmithals being a notable exception) view the individual parts of the letter as closely interrelated, although most are unclear about how the middle section relates to the first. We will then demonstrate that Paul's doctrine of justification by faith is best understood in relation to his doctrine of the inclusion of uncircumcised Gentiles.

F. C. Baur[143] divided the letter into three major parts plus a conclusion with each major part leading naturally into the next. The first part (Chapters 1 and 2) he designated as 'personal and apologetic' consisting primarily of proof of Paul's apostleship and independence in the gospel. This personal vindication led to the second part (Chapters 3 and 4) which he called 'dogmatic'. This consists of proof of the proposition that salvation is by justification by faith in Christ and not by the works of the law. The third part (Gal. 5: 1 – 6: 10) he termed 'hortatory' and 'practical' since it consists of an exhortation to remain in the freedom which the gospel brings followed by a warning against abuse. A final section (Gal. 6: 11–18) which he called the 'conclusion' contains a summary of the letter and a benediction.

Baur considered all the parts to be closely interwoven. He says:

The dogmatic part of the Epistle proceeds, on the one hand, on the vindication that has been given of the writer's apostolic authority, and on the other, it passes naturally over to the practical part, inasmuch as the νόμος is one of the chief ideas of the dogmatic part. It was necessary to show that freedom from the law does not by any means do away with the obligations of moral conduct.[144]

Baur's understanding of the structure of the letter presupposes that the opponents at Galatia were judaizers and that all the letter is either an attack against their theology or a defense against their charges. Schmithals, without denying this basic outline or that there is a continuity of thought between the middle section and the rest of the letter, views the relationship of the individual parts differently.[145] According to him the Galatian heretics, who were gnostics not judaizers, demanded circumcision but not the whole law. As a result Paul reminds the Galatians that the consequence of accepting circumcision is the obligation of keeping the whole law. For Schmithals this means that those parts in the middle section in which the Galatians are not directly addressed (viz., Gal. 3: 6–14; 3: 15–18; 3: 19 – 4: 7; 4: 21–31) consist of nothing more than *topoi* of Paul's discussions and debates with the Jews that the law is no longer valid for Christians. They reveal nothing more about the situation in Galatia than that 'people there in some way were holding to the law'.[146] Therefore the relationship of this section to the rest of the letter is different from what Baur thought. It was not conceived of or written exclusively for the Galatian letter; it is impersonal and intrinsically unrelated to the theology of the opponents.

Furthermore, unlike Baur who explained the third section as Paul's warning against taking freedom from the law as a license to sin, a stricture placed on the possible implications of his preceding remarks, Schmithals views this section as an attack on the libertinism of the gnostics and thus unrelated to the middle part. In other words, according to Schmithals, Paul's section on justification by faith has nothing to do with the theology or the ethics of the opponents or in any other way with the situation in Galatia except that it corrects a misunderstanding of the gospel which, though not admitted by the heretics, is a logical conclusion to their teaching.

But there are reasons to view the middle section as more closely related to the first two chapters than this. Many scholars employing different approaches conclude that the letter is a tightly knit unity. John Bligh,[147] for instance, says that all the sections of the epistle relate to Paul's discourse at Antioch and justify the stand which he took there against Peter. The parts are thus closely interrelated. The Antioch discourse, which was addressed to Peter and to all Jewish Christians at Antioch, incorporates the whole of the second main section of the letter except for Gal. 4: 11–20 and includes 2: 14b (a preliminary protest to Peter), 2: 15 – 3: 4 (the opening section), 3: 5 – 4: 30 (the discourse proper), and 4: 31 – 5: 10a (the concluding section). Paul composed a new ending, 5: 10b–13, to make the discourse appropriate to the Galatians and probably repositioned the original ending at 6: 16–18. He also made a few other revisions, viz., the insertion of 'Galatians' in 3: 1, 'having begun with the Spirit, will you now end with the flesh' in 3: 3b, and some minor changes in 4: 31 – 5: 13.

This understanding of the structure of the middle section affects its interpretation according to Bligh. Since the Antioch discourse was directed to Jewish not Gentile Christians, much of its wording applies to Jewish Christians only. When Paul says in Gal. 3: 13: 'Christ redeemed us from the curse of the law', he means that Christ redeemed 'us Jewish Christians'. When in 3: 24 Paul says: 'The law was our pedagogue unto Christ', he means the law was the pedagogue of the Jewish Christians. And in 4: 5 when Paul says that Christ redeemed those under the law, he means that Christ redeemed Jews, not Gentiles.

R. W. Funk, who approaches the New Testament letters from the point of view of style analysis, concludes that Galatians is a 'tightly conceived unity'.[148] Funk's student, John White, who is concerned primarily with the background of the common Greek letter, gives a more extensive style analysis to Galatians.[149] He says that the body-middle of Galatians, 1: 15 – 4: 31 (minus 4: 12-20), like Romans is composed of two parts. Part I, 1: 15 – 2: 21 'is a tightly organized theological argument'; Part II 'immediately following and extending to the close of the body-middle, is constructed less tightly and is the place where the principles espoused in Part I are further concretized in light of the readers' situation'.[150]

Though it is difficult to agree with White's understanding of the individual parts (i.e., it would appear that a reverse order in the explanations of Parts I and II would be more correct) it is noteworthy that he views the middle section of Galatians as being closely related both to the first part of the letter and to the situation at Galatia itself.

H. D. Betz says that Galatians corresponds in style to the principles of epistolography and rhetoric accepted in Paul's day.[151] In order to demonstrate this he divides the letter into a prescript (1: 1-5), a body (1: 6 - 6: 10), and a postscript (6: 11-18). For the body of the letter he follows the forms laid out in Aristotle, Cicero, and Quintilian.

Independently of Betz, we submit here the following comparison of Galatians with Cicero's *de Inventione*[152] with the addition of a prescript and a postscript: the prescript (1: 1–5), the *exordium* (1: 6–10), the *narratio* (1: 11 – 2: 14), the *partitio* (2: 15–21), the *confirmatio* (3: 1 – 4: 31), the *reprehensio* (5: 1 – 6: 10), and the *conclusio* (which also serves as an epistolary postscript) (6: 11–18). There are of course some deviations in Galatians from the pattern of Cicero. It is particularly noteworthy, however, that Paul's use of emotion apparently follows the rhetorical principle of πάθος according to the tradition of Aristotle and Cicero against Thrasymachus.[153] Thus the emotional references scattered throughout the letter, viz., 1: 8–9; 4: 16, 19; 5: 12; and especially 6: 17, do not indicate that Paul is emotionally disturbed and disjointed in his writing. They seem rather to indicate that he employed the accepted rhetorical device of *movere audientium animos*.

If there is any validity in viewing Galatians as following the patterns of epistolography and rhetoric (perhaps along with other forms)[154] we may conclude that the letter as a whole is a unit and concentrates on one theme. This, of course, does not mean that Paul was bound by any official method of letter-writing or textbook on rhetoric. It is very clear from his deviations from such of these as we know, that he was quite free in his letter-writing. It is much more probable that Paul understood the accepted procedures of epistolography and rhetoric and adapted their principles, perhaps subconsciously, to fit his own needs and style. Nevertheless, it does seem reasonable to assume, on the basis of style alone, that Paul's letter is a thematic unit. This, coupled with the fact that most interpreters, regardless of their approach, view the letter as concentrating on one major theme, causes us to look to the non-circumcised Gentile motif as a key to the middle section.

II

Chapter 3 of Galatians may be outlined (by verses) as follows:

Justification by faith is supported by

1. Experience	1–5
2. Abraham	6–9
3. Scripture	10–14
4. Promise	15–18
5. Law	19–25
6. Unity	26–29

Two examples will be given to show generally how the passage as a whole is interpreted.

(1) Schoeps[155] concentrates on Paul's use of the curse of the law as a key to the passage. According to him Paul's use differs from that of Philo and the Rabbis, who refer to the curse when they wish to describe, mainly

in regard to the advent of the Messiah, the accumulation of sins which characterizes the time. Moreover they balance the curse with the blessings of the law. Paul, on the other hand, uses the curse of the law to demonstrate its unfulfillability, that is, *everyman* stands under the curse since no man is able to do all the law.

Schoeps divides vss. 10–14 into three sequences of thought. First is the concept of common experience expressed by 'it is evident' (δῆλόν ἐστιν). It teaches the impossibility of obtaining righteousness on the basis of the law. 'The tacit underlying assumption' of Deut. 27: 26, Schoeps says, 'is that in fact no man can fulfil the law'.[156] Therefore Paul emphasizes the points that *all* are under the curse and that *all* the law is involved (i.e., the 613 commands and prohibitions) by using the Septuagintal-type text which has the plus readings of 'everyone' (πᾶς) and 'all' (πᾶσιν). Second is Paul's use of the thirteenth *midda* or exegetical principle of Rabbi Ishmael that if two verses contradict each other, a third verse may be used as a solution. To Schoeps, Hab. 2: 4 ('the just shall live by faith') and Lev. 18: 5 ('he who has done them shall live in them') are contradictory since they give two opposing ways to life. Paul resolves the issue by referring back to Gen. 15: 6 ('Abraham believed God and it was reckoned to him as righteousness') in the recapitulated form of the word εὐλογία ('blessing'). Third is Paul's remembrance, at his mention of the curse of the law, of the Jewish offence toward the cross of Christ since it too incurs a curse in accordance with Deut. 21: 23 ('a hanged man is accursed by God'). Paul resolves the problem by reinterpreting the Hebrew *taluy* ('hanged') as 'elevated/exalted', and thereby transforms the curse into a blessing.

Schoeps points to other ways that Paul vitiates the importance of the law. He does so by contrasting the law with the promise and by showing that the promise was fulfilled by Christ not the law. He describes the law as 'a pedagogue unto Christ' and, in a fashion which is perhaps farthest from Rabbinic thought, he indicates that the law derived not from God but from angels.

In summary we may say that Schoeps' analysis emphasizes the inadequacy of the law as a means of salvation. Its unfulfillability, its curse, its origin, and its original purpose all suggest a need for its removal, and by way of contrast, a need for faith in Christ apart from the works of the law as the only viable way to salvation. Thus the doctrine of justification by faith is a doctrine about how man is justified by believing in Christ instead of keeping the law.

(2) The commentary of H. D. McDonald[157] presents another though more recent analysis. He shows an interest in pointing out the inadequacy of the works-principle as a means of salvation and in contrasting it with

the faith-principle. In reference to Abraham's faith he says: 'It is the faith-principle, as against the works-principle, which the story of Abraham makes clear.'[158] The Galatians learn from this that they are sons of Abraham by just believing 'because their lives are based on and ordered by the same faith-principle as Abraham's'.[159] The advantage of salvation by faith, to Jews and Gentiles alike, is that it provides a way of escape from the curse of the law which comes to those who depend on the law, 'unless every detail of the law is fulfilled and every ordinance kept'.[160] This of course is an impossible task: 'For who can render with entire exactitude and satisfaction the least of the law's demands, much less its weightier precepts? None.'[161] Moreover: 'Whatever its provisions, whether ceremonial or moral, all must be fully met; whoever fails in one requirement is constituted by the law as a 'transgressor', and is consequently "cursed".'[162]

According to McDonald, Christ became a curse for all men including Gentiles, since all were under the curse of the law. And since Christ's redemptive act all men, including Gentiles, are justified by faith. 'Since it is "by faith", as is proved in the case of Abraham, and not by adherence to law, then the blessing is open to all Gentiles.'[163]

These two examples, though differing in detail, reflect an understanding of Galatians 3 which is held by many interpreters. This understanding may be described in the following way: The law in Paul's mind demanded complete obedience and taught that one infraction of a command brought with it a curse. As a remedy for this impossible way to life God provided Jesus Christ as a redeemer and now all who believe in him are justified by their faith. Paul argues for faith as the only means of salvation by pointing to the experience of the Galatians, that they received the Spirit by the hearing of faith and not by the works of the law (Gal. 3: 1-5), by the example *par excellence* of Abraham who was justified by faith (6-9), by his quotations from Scripture to prove the law's unfulfillability and the divine sanction of faith in Jesus Christ (10-14), and generally by showing the inferiority of the law to faith (15-29).

In our analysis of this explanation we will attempt to show that there are two questionable presuppositions connected with it. First, at its basis is the belief that Paul's concern is with a dichotomy between works and faith. Works supposedly imply a system of merit in which a man is justified by keeping the law. Faith, on the other hand, supposedly excludes works by definition and belongs to a system of grace. Faith and works are considered to be opposite ways to righteousness and are in fact incompatible. As one has so clearly put it: 'The whole matter is now on a different plane – believing instead of achieving.'[164]

The problem with this is that alongside this common assumption is the equally common recognition that Jewish Christianity continued to keep the law while it submitted to justification by faith. Schoeps, for instance, speaks of the moderate Jerusalem group into which Peter and James fit, which held to the observance of the law for the Jews, although it made concessions in this regard to the Gentiles.[165] Another recent interpreter says:

> Even in Galatians, his most uncompromising deliverance on the subject, his concern is solely with the imposing of circumcision on Gentile Christians; whether Jewish Christians continued to circumcise their children or not was probably a matter of small importance in his eyes, on a par with their continued observance or non-observance of the sabbath and the Levitical food-laws.[166]

But the coexistence of works of law and faith in Christ in Jewish Christianity suggests that the two are not absolutely incompatible from the standpoint of early Christianity. To argue that the law was done away because it demanded the impossible task of legal purity, and that to accept circumcision was to assume the obligation of this impossible task and to nullify the effects of faith in Christ is out of harmony with the facts. If Jewish Christianity practised the law while accepting faith in Jesus Christ as the way to salvation, how can it be said that the early church, including Paul, considered the two as mutually exclusive principles of life?

It may be argued that Jewish Christianity continued to observe the law *only* out of custom[167] or a desire for good citizenship[168] or on behalf of the Jewish mission,[169] but not as a means to righteousness, and for this reason the observance of the law did not nullify faith in Christ. But if law-keeping is compatible with faith when it is observed only for practical reasons, why did Paul not explain to the Galatians that it was all right to observe the law just so long as one did not observe it as a *sine qua non* for salvation? Why did he not permit circumcision for the sake of unity which was a very important practical matter at that time? After all the Galatians were already in Christ and redeemed from the law's curse so that observances of the law for mere practical reasons should incur no guilt if they were imperfect in their performance of it. And also there was Abraham who, as the Galatians knew from the Genesis account, accepted circumcision after his initial faith in God and that his acceptance of it in no way nullified the efficacy of his faith. Since Paul supposedly used him as *the* example of justification by faith why did he not proceed to show that, like Abraham, the Galatians would be perfectly safe from legal obligations if they submitted to circumcision after their initial justification?

The conclusion is inescapable that if Jewish Christianity continued to keep the law, and the evidence of the New Testament shows that it did, there is nothing incompatible in faith in Christ and works of the law when each is kept in its proper place. But in spite of this, the Galatian letter fails to present one shred of evidence that Paul reasoned this way or that such possibilities ever entered into his mind. Paul's prohibition of the law is so absolute and irrevocable that he leaves open no conceivable occasion when Gentiles might submit to circumcision and be saved. His preclusion of circumcision to the Galatians under any circumstances,[170] in spite of the fact that from his meeting with the Jerusalem 'pillars' he obviously knew that they would continue to observe the law, strongly suggests that his concern was not with the incompatibility of the principles of faith and works but rather and *only* with the notion of Gentiles accepting circumcision and the Mosaic law. In Paul's mind the law of Moses, though suitable for the Jewish Christians, would damn the Gentiles if they tried to keep it.

Second, this interpretation assumes that in Paul's mind the law required absolute obedience and that one infraction of its legal demands resulted in a curse. Lindars says that Paul's purpose in quoting Deut. 27: 26 is 'to show that the Law is not the means of salvation. Because it is humanly impossible to keep it in its fulness, it only has the effect of bringing a curse.'[171] Bligh says: 'He took it in the strictest possible sense as meaning that any Jew who broke any written law came under this curse.'[172]

The problem with this assumption is that Paul, who by his own admission knew the law well (Gal. 1: 14), knew that the cultic aspect of the law implied the imperfection of man. The Levitical system of sacrifices provided a means whereby man, when he sinned, could obtain forgiveness. In fact observance of the law to a large degree involved the offering of sacrifices for the atonement of sins. To keep the law then was, among other things, to find cultic forgiveness for breaking the law. For Paul to have argued that the law demanded absolute obedience and that one legal infraction brought with it unpardonable doom, would have been for him to deny what all the world knew, namely, that the Jerusalem temple stood as a monument to the belief that Yahweh was a forgiving God who pardoned his people when they sinned.[173]

In our view, the traditional interpretation of the chapter needs to be re-examined. In addition to its questionable presuppositions it also fails to correlate well with the theme of the inclusion of uncircumcised Gentiles. This is a very notable failure since it is this theme which dominates the first two chapters of the letter. While most observe that Paul relates his doctrine of faith to the Gentiles, few deal at length with the subject. Generally the passage is held to be a discussion of salvation theories with faith winning out as the best. The argument is that faith has replaced works and since people can now be saved, Gentiles can be saved. But beyond this little is said about Paul's doctrine of the inclusion of uncircumcised Gentiles in relation to his teachings on faith.

III

The discovery of the Dead Sea Scrolls and the recent increase in Septuagint[174] and Targum[175] studies has given rise to a better understanding of the use of Old Testament quotations in the New. The pesher quotations in the Qumran documents and in general the midrashic[176] world of Jewish hermeneutics show that the writers of that time exercised freedom in their use of the Old Testament text. This freedom involved, among other things, the selection of variant readings, the adoption of *ad hoc* texts, quotations in abbreviated forms, and oblique inferences from apparently unrelated passages. It is now also clear that the New Testament writers used the Old Testament text in much the same way.[177]

The relevance of this for our purposes is that the third chapter of Galatians hangs upon the structure of seven Old Testament quotations. These are: (1) vs. 6 – Gen. 15: 6 ('Abraham believed God and it was reckoned to him for righteousness'), (2) vs. 8 – Gen. 12: 3 ('In thee shall all the nations be blessed'), (3) vs. 10 – Deut. 27: 26 ('Cursed is everyone who does not remain in all things written in the book of the law to do them'), (4) vs. 11 – Hab. 2: 4 ('The just shall live by faith'), (5) vs. 12 – Lev. 18: 5 ('The one who has done them shall live in them'), (6) vs. 13 – Deut. 21: 23 ('Cursed is everyone who hangs on a tree'), and (7) vs. 16 – Gen. 12: 7/13: 15/24: 7 ('And to your seed'). The text of Nos. 1, 2, 5, 6, and 7 is basically that of the Septuagint with occasional though minor differences from the Masoretic Text. No. 3 differs from both the Septuagint and the Masoretic Text but shows Septuagintal influence. No. 4 differs slightly from both the Septuagint and the Masoretic Text.

It is generally assumed that Gen. 15: 6 (vs. 6), which appears also in Rom. 4: 3, sets the stage for Paul's argument that justification is by faith apart from works. Abraham is *the* example of justification; as he believed and was justified without works, so it is with man now.[178] Lindars argues that Paul's logic rules out works by the fact that Gen. 15: 6 comes before the account of Abraham's later acts of hospitality to strangers and the sacrifice of Isaac recorded in Gen. 18 and 22. Moreover, his subsequent quotation of Gen. 12: 3 (vs. 8) extends the promise to the Gentiles who also must have faith without works.[179] It is noteworthy that this places Paul in conflict with the customary usage of Abraham in Jewish literature which employs him as an example of one whose faith, accompanied by works, was itself an attainment.[180]

But it is to be doubted that Paul uses Abraham only as an example. His emphasis on the sons of Abraham (vss. 7, 29) and the blessing of Abraham (vs. 14) suggests that Abraham, rather than being merely an example of justification by faith, is part of a salvific faith-process which works for the salvation of the Gentiles.[181] This point is made clearer in Romans 4 where Abraham is said to be an heir of the cosmos (vs. 13) and a father of many nations (vs. 17). In Gal. 3: 8 ('In thee will all the nations be blessed') and 3: 14 ('that the blessing of Abraham might come unto the Gentiles') the same idea is present. The idea is that the Gentiles are blessed not simply like Abraham but because of Abraham.

Moreover, it is a misunderstanding of the text to make Gal. 3: 6 ('Just as Abraham believed God') the primary content of Abraham's role in the context; the chapter as a whole is an elaboration on the implications of the promise in 3: 8 ('In thee will all the nations be blessed'). Thus vs. 14 concerns the promise and the Gentiles; vss. 15–25 demonstrate the law's role as separate and apart from the promise; and vss. 26–9 show the resultant unity of the promise, namely, the inclusion of the Gentiles as equal partners with the Jews. The quotation of Gal. 3: 6 is never mentioned again and offers nothing further beyond its immediate purpose.

The immediate purpose of this quotation is not simply to begin a new thought as some suppose.[182] Rather it serves as a transitional statement with the primary function of giving an answer in the form of an analogy to the question stated in vs. 5. The question is: 'Therefore the one who supplies (ἐπιχορηγῶν) to you the Spirit and works (ἐνεργῶν) miracles among you, does he do it by works of the law or by the hearing of faith?' It is important to note that the question concerns the activity of God, not that of the Galatians. It is to be expected, then, that the answer will concern the activity of God as well. The answer comes in vs. 6: 'Just as Abraham believed God and it was reckoned (ἐλογίσθη) to him for righteousness.' It would be incorrect to understand this answer to mean that as the Galatians believed so Abraham believed. Often it is taken this way with the conclusion being that the way of salvation is thus proven to be by faith rather than works. The point of the quotation, however, is to be sought in another direction. The point is: As God 'supplies' and 'works' to and among the Galatians, so he 'reckoned' to Abraham.

In Rom. 4: 3 Paul quotes this same passage with the following explanatory remarks:[183] 'Now to the one who works the reward is not reckoned (λογίζεται) according to grace but according to debt. But to the one who does not work, but believes on the one who justifies the ungodly, his faith is reckoned (λογίζεται) unto righteousness' (vss. 4–6). It is thought that Paul here deviates from the Jewish position of seeing in Abraham's faith an attainment. Paul supposedly sets the faith of Abraham against any works he might have performed.[184] In other words, it is thought that Paul establishes Abraham's justification according to grace by referring to the fact that he merely believed. Faith is supposed to evoke in Paul's mind the concept of 'grace'.

But it does not seem reasonable that Paul would attempt to prove 'grace' by the word 'faith' when the word 'faith', as used by his contemporaries, implied attainment. To construe Paul in this way is to have him base his argument on a reasoning which no one could accept. In any case, a look at the context makes it doubtful that this is Paul's point anyway. He begins with a simple conditional sentence[185] whose fulfillment he leaves open: 'For if Abraham was justified by works, he has a boast, but not toward God.' Paul concedes the possibility that Abraham has a boast on the basis of his works; he only denies that he has a boast before God.[186] Therefore, he does not remove himself entirely from the normal Jewish position. Furthermore, the word in the quotation which stands behind Paul's argument for grace is more naturally understood as 'reckoned' than 'believed'. In Paul's mind 'to reckon' (λογίζεσθαι), used in the absolute state as in Gen. 15: 6, apparently means 'to reckon according to grace' (λογίζεσθαι κατὰ χάριν),[187] his reasoning being that Scripture would have stated explicitly 'to reckon according to debt' (λογίζεσθαι κατὰ ὀφείλημα) if obligation had been involved. Paul considered λογίζεσθαι by itself to be equivalent to 'give freely' (χαρίζεσθαι).[188] This means that Paul argues for a dichotomy between works and faith in Abraham's case not because works and faith customarily and automatically imply opposite ways to salvation, but because in the particular case of Abraham's faith Scripture employs the absolute use of λογίζεσθαι. Abraham had righteousness *reckoned* to him and this means that it was by grace.

The analogous case of David, which Paul mentions next (Rom. 4: 6-8), shows that this is the probable interpretation. Paul says that David pronounces a blessing on the man to whom God 'reckons' righteousness apart from works. The Scripture that he quotes from David is Ps. 32: 1-2: 'Blessed are those whose iniquities are forgiven, and whose sins are covered; blessed is the man whose sin the Lord will not reckon (μὴ λογίσηται)'. It is noteworthy that neither 'works' nor 'faith' appears in the quotation. This means that neither of these words figures in his proof. Clearly the reason Paul takes the pronouncement as a bestowal of grace is because God forgives the man of his sins, not because the man is said to have faith apart from works. The last clause employing λογίζεσθαι is placed in synonymous parallelism with God's forgiveness showing the force of λογίζεσθαι when used in the absolute state.[189] Thus the 'grace' motif in Paul's use of Abraham throughout this chapter is predicated on the concept of God's 'reckoning', not on Abraham's 'believing'.

In Gal. 3: 6 the emphasis likewise rests upon the word 'reckon'. The purpose of the verse is not to illustrate that man is justified by his faith apart from his works, but to illustrate that salvation derives from God alone. Here we must be very clear because such language is customarily used to mean that salvation is by the grace of God when it is appropriated by man's faith. 'Faith' in this sense usually means 'faith apart from works', a notion which we are trying to show is not in view in the present context. What Paul means is that justification is *solely* from God apart from any human activity including both faith and works, and since the Mosaic law is something for man to perform it cannot possibly figure in the justification of the Galatians. Just as Abraham had righteousness reckoned to him (as an act of pure grace) so the Galatians have had righteousness reckoned to them. This Paul uses to support his doctrine of the inclusion of uncircumcised Gentiles, not to separate man's faith from his works.

The quotation now forms an introduction to the following verses which show that the inclusion of the Gentiles was first formulated as a promise from God to Abraham. The promise was: 'In thee shall all the nations be blessed.' Paul argues from this that the law can play no role in the justification of the Gentiles because their justification is solely a matter of God *keeping faith* with his promise, not a matter of something they themselves do.

The relationship of vs. 6 with vss. 7ff. is two-fold. The first and most important connection between them is the concept of grace. As Abraham was justified by grace so were the Gentiles justified. God ushered them into the kingdom in fulfillment of the promise as a pure act of grace. The second and less important connection between them is the appearance of the words 'believed' in vs. 6 and 'those out of faith' in vss. 7 and 9. This is a word-connection relationship only that serves to give a literary flavor to the flow of the argument.[190] 'Those out of faith' are not those who simply 'believe' like Abraham 'believed', but those who have been justified by God's grace. They are described as 'those out of faith' because they belong to the faith-act of God which fulfilled the promise. It is from this context that vs. 8 derives its meaning: 'And the Scripture, foreseeing that God would justify the Gentiles by faith ($\dot{\epsilon}\kappa$ $\pi\acute{\iota}\sigma\tau\epsilon\omega\varsigma$), preached beforehand the gospel to Abraham, saying, "all the Gentiles shall be blessed in you".' It is not that the Gentiles would be justified if *they* had faith, but rather that *God* would justify them by faith, that is, by his faith-act toward the promise that all the Gentiles would be blessed in Abraham.

This divine faith-act forms an important concept in Paul's doctrine of justification by faith. In Gal. 2: 16 he speaks of it in his discourse with

Peter when he says that 'man is not justified by the works of the law, but through the faith of Jesus Christ (διὰ πίστεως Ἰησοῦ Χριστοῦ) and we believed (ἐπιστεύσαμεν) on Christ Jesus in order that we might be justified by the faith of Christ (ἐκ πίστεως Χριστοῦ) and not by the works of the law'. The argument is that non-circumcised Gentiles are to be accepted by Jewish Christians like Peter because no man is justified by the works of the law, but only by the faith-act of Christ. In Gal. 3: 22 a similar notion is stated: 'The Scripture shut up all under sin in order that the promise by the faith of Jesus Christ (ἐκ πίστεως Ἰησοῦ Χριστοῦ) might be given to those who believe.'

The traditional view of faith is concerned primarily with those passages which speak of faith in Christ. The idea is that if man believes in Christ he will be saved. But there are other aspects of faith which are temporally and causally antecedent to the Christian's faith. In Rom. 3: 3, for example, Paul speaks of the faith of God (τὴν πίστιν τοῦ θεοῦ) which is operative in spite of man's lack of faith. In Rom. 4: 16 Paul speaks of the 'faith of Abraham' (πίστεως Αβραάμ) in terms of making the promise secure for all nations. It is within this sphere of thought that he speaks of the 'faith of Christ'.[191] The idea is that Christ fulfills the divine pledge to bless the Gentiles by bringing all nations into the kingdom of God. The purpose of this act is to bring the nations out of idolatry into acceptance of Yahweh as the only true God. As we will see this concept forms a key to the confusing verses about the relationship of law and faith which follow.

Paul's discussion of the curse of the law in Gal. 3: 10–14 involves a cluster of four quotations, viz., Deut. 27: 26 (vs. 10), Hab. 2: 4 (vs. 11), Lev. 18: 5 (vs. 12), and Deut. 21: 23 (vs. 13). The first and the last obviously belong together. Vs. 10 states that all are under a curse; vs. 13 states that Christ became a curse for us. Lindars argues that Paul's combination of these two quotations reflects an early Christian apologetic which contrasted Christ's condemnation and his resurrection, the latter proving him innocent. In Paul, he says, a further step is made in that Christ, by becoming a curse for us, made an atonement for sins.[192]

The connection of vs. 13, which speaks of the atoning death of Christ, with vs. 10 is, from another point of view, problematic since the two in combination imply that those whom Christ redeemed from the law are *only* those under the law. On the surface, at least, this means that Christ redeemed the Jews only. It is not surprising, therefore, to find wide differences of opinion over this point. Some argue that 'us' in vs. 13 means only Jewish Christians.[193] Robinson attempts to distinguish systematically between Jewish and Gentile Christians in Galatians and says about this verse: 'Those whom Christ redeemed through his death from the curse of

the law were *Jews*. The Gentile Galatians are not included in the "us" of
the first sentence.'[194] A host of others argue that vs. 13 includes all men
in Christ's redemption though there is little agreement on how it does.[195]

The answer to this problem may lie in the type of text Paul quotes in
vs. 10. His quotation corresponds roughly to the Septuagint. But it varies
in at least two significant plus readings from the Hebrew. The additions are
'everyone' ($\pi \hat{\alpha} \varsigma$) and 'all' ($\pi \hat{\alpha} \sigma \iota \nu$). The second of these two variants has
been used to support the popular belief in the unfulfillability of the law.
One interpreter, for example, says: 'This addition is essential to Paul's
argument that if a man is going to base his salvation upon his obedience to
the law, there can be no exception, even for the least of its commandments.
He must keep them all, for he will be as fatally cursed for a small as for a
great infraction.'[196] In other words, the purpose of Paul's form of the
quotation, according to this view, is to point out that any infraction, great
or small, is fatal. We have already noted the weakness of this interpretation
and need not be detained further with it. Nevertheless Paul's addition is
emphatic, and, as we will argue later, has an effect on the context.

However, Paul's addition of 'everyone' ($\pi \hat{\alpha} \varsigma$) is of immediate significance
since it implies that everyone is under the law. This means that vs. 13, which
speaks of redemption from the curse of the law, applies to all men, both
Jews and Gentiles.[197] As problematic as this first appears it is certainly the
position which Paul takes. This is made clear by his subsequent discussion.
In vs. 22 he says that 'the Scripture shut up all ($\tau \grave{\alpha} \pi \acute{\alpha} \nu \tau \alpha$) under sin'. The
only Scripture to which this can refer is Gal. 3: 10, since it is the only one
in the entire letter that states this premise. Vss. 23–26 reflect the same
point of view. 'But before the faith came *we* were kept under the law... so
that the law is become *our* pedagogue unto Christ... But since the faith
has come, *we* are no longer under a pedagogue. For *you* all are sons of God
through the faith in Christ Jesus.' The most natural way to understand the
alternation of the pronouns is that Paul made no distinction in Jews and
Gentiles, but included all men within the purview of his words. The sequence
of verses in Gal. 4: 4–6 continues in the same way: 'God sent forth his son
... in order to redeem those under the law in order that *we* might receive
the adoption. And because *you* are sons God sent forth the Spirit of his son
into *our* hearts.' Again the pronouns show that Paul has both Jew and Gentile under consideration.[198]

This same thought emerges in Romans. In Rom. 6: 14 Paul says: 'For
sin shall not reign over you, for you are not under the law but under grace.'
There is absolutely nothing in the context to imply that these words were
spoken only to Jews; they naturally apply to all his readers. Later he says:

So that, my brothers, also *you* were made dead to the law through the body of Christ in order that *you* might belong to another, to the one who was raised from the dead in order that *we* might bear fruit to God. For when *we* were in the flesh the passions of sins which were through the law, worked in *our* members in order to bear fruit to death; but now *we* have been discharged from the law, having died to that in which *we* were held, so that *we* serve in newness of the Spirit and not in oldness of the letter (Rom. 7: 4–6).

There can be no doubt that Paul spoke these words to all alike without distinction between Jew and Gentile.

The question that arises in all of this is: in what way can it be said that the Gentiles were ever under the law? The Jews could be said to be under the law in that they were subjected to its commandments by birth. Some Gentiles came under the law in a similar way by entering Judaism as proselytes. But the Gentiles as a whole were not under the law in this sense. In the next chapter we will see that some explain the situation of the Gentiles in terms of the law of nature. They argue that Paul considered the Jews and the Gentiles to be in an analogous position in that both were under some law. This view denies that the Gentiles were directly under the law of Moses. But in the context of Gal. 3: 10 the opposite seems to be Paul's point. His quotation of Deut. 27: 26 makes it clear that it is under the law of Moses that he considered all men to have existed, not just under the concept of law.

This leaves us with the problem of explaining how the Gentiles were under the law of Moses. In our view the reason this problem exists is because the concept of 'being under the Jewish law' usually has only one meaning in modern thought. It is usually understood to mean to be subject to the law's specific demands. This meaning makes perfectly good sense when applied to Jews and Jewish proselytes. But when it is applied to the Gentiles it makes little sense since the Gentiles were not subject to the specific demands of the law of Moses. Therefore a different interpretation is necessary to explain Paul's words.

In the first place we should note carefully Paul's exact words. In Gal. 3: 10 he speaks of those who are 'of the works of the law'. In 3: 13 he says that 'Christ redeemed us from the curse of the law'. In 3: 23 he speaks of the time before the coming of faith as a time in which 'we were kept in ward under the law'. In 4: 5 he says that Christ came 'in order to redeem those under the law'. Such statements do not necessarily convey the notion that to be under the law means to be subject to the specific demands of the law. The tenor of the whole context is one of being restrained, suppressed and cursed under the law.

In our view Paul's concept of being under the law, at least in the present context, is not to be understood in the traditional way. Paul's argument is not that all men are subject to the specific demands of the Jewish law. Paul's thought rather is that the law is a suppressor and a restrainer of mankind. To be *under* the law in this sense means to be *suppressed under the law.* Paul's whole discussion of the law in this section of Galatians aims at showing that the law suppressed the Gentiles and kept them from entering the kingdom of God in an uncircumcised and non-law-abiding state. Consequently, when Paul says that 'Christ redeemed us from the curse of the law', and immediately adds 'in order that the blessing of Abraham might come unto the Gentiles' (vss. 13–14), his thought is that Christ, for the sake of universal unity, redeemed all men, including uncircumcised Gentiles, from the discriminating suppression of the law. When uncircumcised Gentiles were admitted into the kingdom on equal terms with the Jews, universal unity was achieved and the tyranny of the law came to an end.

This point is also very important for Paul's understanding of the redemption of the Jews from the law. Often it is thought that the Jews were redeemed from the law in that the law was done away, brought to an end and literally rescinded. This understanding is fostered by the traditional views that faith in Christ and works of law are mutually incompatible and that one infraction of the law spells unpardonable doom to those who try to keep it. We have already discarded both of these views as untenable. Moreover, the evidence of the New Testament fails to suggest that Christ's act was performed in order to rescind the law of Moses.[199] There are in fact good reasons to argue against this position. First, Paul's acceptance of the agreements at Jerusalem (Gal. 2: 1–10) implies that he understood that the Jerusalem church would continue to practise the law. The concession granted at Jerusalem was that the Gentiles would be free from circumcision, not the Jews.[200] Second, in the Book of Acts this becomes even clearer. The Jerusalem conference (Acts 15) and subsequent events (especially Acts 21: 20–26) show that the understanding in the early church was that although the Gentiles were free from the law the Jews (including Paul) would continue to keep it. This means that although the Jews were redeemed from the law they were not exempted from keeping the law. The law of Moses was as much their law after Christ's redemption as before.

But if Jewish Christianity continued to observe the law, it is necessary to seek for another explanation for its redemption from the law than the traditional view that the law was rescinded. The most natural solution is that the Jews were redeemed from the law precisely in the same sense as the Gentiles. They were redeemed from the suppressing force of the law which separated Jew from Gentile and held back the universal unity which was destined to come.[201] In our judgment the context points to this sense, and to none other, that all men, both Jews and Gentiles, were redeemed from the law.[202] In Christ's redemptive act the law lost its divisive power and uncircumcised Gentiles were ushered into God's kingdom on equal terms with the Jews.[203] This was salvation for Paul, for in that moment Yahweh became the God of all men, and all men became his people.[204]

The unity which Christ's act created could not have come through the law for two reasons: first, because the law divided mankind;[205] second, because God's blessing on the Gentiles was in the form of a promise. This precluded the law as the means of salvation since the promise was for God alone to fulfill.[206]

It may be that the second plus reading in Gal. 3: 10, 'all' ($\pi\tilde{\alpha}\sigma\iota\nu$), has relevance at this point. This emphatic word places a restriction on the possible argument that the law was God's way of fulfilling the promise. By reading $\pi\tilde{\alpha}\sigma\iota\nu$ Paul emphasizes that all the law, not just part of it, is man's responsibility, thus removing any possibility of a counter argument that the law's obligation was partly man's and partly God's, or perhaps God's altogether.[207] This point is strengthened further when he later adds that the law was ordained by angels (Gal. 3: 19), and so removes God even from its direct enactment.

The two middle quotations in our cluster of four involve further textual variation. The first quotation, Hab. 2: 4 (vs. 11 – 'The just shall live by faith'), appears also in Rom. 1: 17,[208] Heb. 10: 38, and IQp Hab. Paul's form of it varies from all known manuscripts and versions of the text by the omission of the pronoun 'his' or 'my'. The relevant textual evidence is: (1) *MT, Kaige,* IQp Hab (vid) read: 'The just shall live by *his* faith'; (2) *LXX*MSS, Heb. 10: 38D read: 'The just shall live by *my* faith'; (3) *LXX*AC, Heb. 10:38 $\mathfrak{P}$46 א AH read: '*My* just one shall live by faith'; and (4) Gal. 3: 11, Rom. 1: 17 read: 'The just shall live by faith.' In all probability the original reading is either 'by his faith' (באמונתו) or 'by my faith' (באמונתי) since *Yodh* and *Waw* were often identical in ancient Hebrew manuscripts and easily confused. The readings in the majority of witnesses in Heb. 10: 38, following *LXX* AC,[209] and in Paul are almost certainly secondary. Paul may have dropped the pronoun in order to adapt the text to the needs of his argument.[210] The quotation with the pronoun attached to 'faith' implies the mode of conduct one who is already just will pursue, viz., 'The just will live by *his/my* faith.' This is probably the original meaning of the statement in Habakkuk. Paul, on the other hand, wishes to describe how one will obtain salvation-life; his answer is: 'The one who is justified by faith will find eternal life.'

J. A. Sanders compares Paul's use of Hab. 2: 4 with IQp Hab and says that the major difference in the two is that IQp Hab, in accordance with normative Judaism, teaches that righteousness comes by faithfully doing the works of the law; Paul, on the other hand, teaches that it comes by having faith in the person of Christ.[211] A slightly different view is presented by Bruce who, copying the pesher idiom of the Qumran documents, explains Paul's meaning as follows: 'Its interpretation concerns the man who has faith in Jesus, for his faith is reckoned to him for righteousness, and he will receive the life of the age to come.'[212] He notes further that this personal direction of faith is paralleled in IQp Hab where the men of truth are said to be those whom God 'will save from the house of judgment (i.e., will justify) because of their faith in (or loyalty to) the Righteous Teacher'.[213] In spite of their differences both suggest that Paul uses Hab. 2: 4 to teach faith in Jesus Christ.

But there are reasons to object to this view. In the immediate context there is no reference to faith in Christ. Gal. 3: 14 ends with: 'That we might receive the promise of the Spirit through *the* faith (διὰ τῆς πίστεως)', an obvious reference back to vs. 11; but there is no mention of faith in Christ. Moreover to understand Paul's use of Hab. 2: 4 as a reference to faith in Christ creates a problem with the next words: 'But the law is not of faith.' It is hardly conceivable that Paul would argue that the law is not of faith because it is not based on Jesus Christ. This would go without saying. Given Paul's emphasis on Abraham's faith, which likewise had nothing to do with faith in Jesus Christ, Paul would be very unconvincing in any attempt to eliminate the law simply for not resting on faith in Christ.

But what does Paul mean when he says the law is not of faith? Lightfoot explains: 'Faith is not the starting-point of the law. The law does not take faith as its fundamental principle.'[214] Schlier says: 'The law is not "out of faith", it does not have faith as a basic principle of its life.'[215] Mussner says: 'The law-principle does not spring up "out of faith".'[216] But is it proper to ascribe such an argument to the apostle when it must have been clear to all that faith was the very warp and woof of the law? The whole law and the Prophets were fundamentally and primarily concerned with faith in God with all that that implied, including loyalty, trust, commitment and absolute submission to his sovereignty. Paul would have been laughed off the scene even to have suggested a contrary notion.

But it is possible to understand the passage in a way that precludes this abrasive point of view. Paul's quotation of Lev. 18: 5 in connection with the Habakkuk passage does not contrast man's faith in Christ with his works. The contrast is rather between man's works (including his faith) and God's faithful act in fulfilling the promise. The law 'is not of faith' *only* in the sense that it is non-promissory and consequently beyond God's duty to perform it. The whole context is governed by the concept of the promise of God to bless the Gentiles. The law could never be his way of fulfilling the promise because the law in its entirety demanded fulfillment from man. The promise, on the other hand, in its entirety demanded fulfillment from God. This means that the promise could only be fulfilled by God by his ushering the uncircumcised Gentile world into the kingdom.[217]

Gal. 3: 13-14 take us a step further by telling us how this promise was kept. Christ, as God's administrator of the divine faith, fulfilled God's commitment by redeeming man from the curse of the law. Paul does not explain in detail how Christ's act was for our benefit (a normal procedure for Paul); only the context gives the meaning. The redemption of mankind was a redemption from the law's tyranny of division. The law, by its divisive power, suppressed the nations and kept Israel in isolation. Christ's unification thus was a redemption from the law in order to form a unity between Jew and Gentile. In this view, Paul's doctrine of justification by faith is the doctrine that God has included uncircumcised Gentiles into the kingdom as an act of divine faith to the promise given to Abraham.

The last quotation, Gen. 12: 7, 13: 15, 24: 7 ('And to your seed'), comes in the next paragraph (Gal. 3: 15-20) which makes a contrast between the law and the promise. First, the promise was spoken to Abraham and to his seed, which, by a bit of Jewish hermeneutics, Paul interprets as Christ; only to Abraham and to Christ was the promise given. This eliminates the Jewish race from being *the* seed of Abraham and the official recipients of the promise. Second, the promise is made analogous to a $\delta\iota\alpha\vartheta\dot{\eta}\kappa\eta$[218] (covenant or testament). Once a $\delta\iota\alpha\vartheta\dot{\eta}\kappa\eta$ is ratified no one can annul it or add to it. Since the promise to Abraham came 430 years before the law, the law cannot annul or add to it. A logic stands behind Paul's words at this point since by nature the law and the promise are opposites. The law is incumbent on man to perform; the promise is incumbent on God to perform. Therefore, the law can play no role in the promise: 'For if the inheritance is by the law, it is no longer by promise; but God gave it to Abraham by a promise' (Gal. 3: 18). The law, on the other hand, was given because of transgressions until the seed should come (vs. 19).

The function and temporality of the law receive elaboration in vss. 21-5. Paul says that the law is not against God's promises. Rather the Scripture (probably Deut. 27: 26; cf. Gal. 3: 10) shut up all under sin 'that the promise *by the faith of Jesus Christ* ($\dot{\epsilon}\kappa$ $\pi\dot{\iota}\sigma\tau\epsilon\omega\varsigma$ $'I\eta\sigma\upsilon\tilde{\upsilon}$ $X\rho\iota\sigma\tau\upsilon\tilde{\upsilon}$) might be given to those who believe' (Gal. 3: 22). The law, in contrast to the promise, closed up man under sin. The fulfillment of the promise, on the other hand, came through the faithful act of Jesus Christ. Before this faith (τὴν πίστιν; Gal. 3: 23) came the law was a restraining pedagogue. But now that the faith has been kept we are no longer under the law. The purpose? 'In order that we might be justified by faith' (Gal. 3: 24).

This 'faith' is the faith of Christ, who, by keeping the promise given to Abraham, brought salvation to non-law-abiding Gentiles and unity to mankind. In the concluding verses (Gal. 3: 26–9) the apostle spells out this unity.

> For you are all sons of God through this faith in Christ Jesus.[219] For as many of you as were baptized into Christ put on Christ. There is neither Jew nor Greek; there is neither bond nor free; there is neither male nor female; for you are all one in Christ Jesus. And if you are Christ's, then you are Abraham's seed, heirs according to the promise.

Thus we have seen that the context of the chapter as a whole deals with the inclusion of uncircumcised Gentiles. The problem with which the apostle wrestles is the idea of one God over a pagan world. How is it that God can bring the nations out of idolatry to faith in him? The process is two-fold: first, the promise that all nations will be blessed is given to Abraham; second, the promise is fulfilled by Christ. Justification by faith, then, is the inclusion of all nations, apart from the works of the law, into the kingdom of God in fulfillment to the promise.

The faithful act of Christ had effect on both Jews and Gentiles, for the law had divided them into hostile camps. The dividing force of the law, holding back the unity which was destined to come, suppressed all men under the law. Christ's redemption from the law was a redemption of all men for the sake of unity; or as the apostle puts it: 'In order that the blessing of Abraham might come on the Gentiles in Christ Jesus.'

The whole context transports us away from the modern notion of faith versus works. This concept has served to cover up the real meaning of the chapter which has to do with Paul's doctrine of the inclusion of uncircumcised Gentiles. When it is seen that Paul's argument does not envision the modern distinctions commonly made between human activity and human faith, a different picture emerges. Paul's argument distinguishes justification by man (including his works, faith, and any other conceivable human act) from justification by God. Justification for Paul is a pure act of grace which created unity among all nations under one God. When this happened the law lost its power of division and the Gentiles and the Jews alike accepted Yahweh as the God of all men.

4

PAUL'S VIEW OF THE LAW

In the previous chapter certain aspects of the law were delineated in the discussion of Paul's view of justification by faith. In the present chapter we consider the specific issue of Paul's view of the law in relation to the 'elements of the world' (τὰ στοιχεῖα τοῦ κόσμου). After reviewing some key interpretations of the meaning of this phrase and its use in the context we will reinterpret the passage in terms of Paul's view of the inclusion of uncircumcised Gentiles into the kingdom of God. It will be our contention that Paul looked upon that version of Christianity propagated by the juda-izers as synonymous with paganism since it made Yahweh into the national God of Israel only. The gospel as Paul preached it demanded a continued ethnic distinctiveness between Jews and Gentiles in order that Yahweh, the God of the Hebrews, could be conceptualized by both Jews and Gentiles as the God of all nations.

I

In Gal. 4: 3 Paul says: 'Thus also we, when we were babes were enslaved to the elements of the world.' Just what Paul means by 'the elements of the world' is problematic and has been the source of endless debate. Without entering into a lengthy discussion of the derivation and history of the word 'elements' (στοιχεῖα), since this has been done often and well in the past,[220] it is sufficient to say that originally στοιχεῖον meant 'what belongs to a series or a row'. Later στοιχεῖα came to be used in reference to the 'elements' of anything or its 'basic principles'. Thus in 2 Pet. 3: 10 the word possibly refers to the material elements of the universe which will be consumed at the day of the Lord. In Heb. 5: 12 it apparently stands for the elementary teachings or principles of the oracles of God.

In Gal. 4: 3 the 'elements of the world' seem most naturally to refer to the elements of the universe, a common usage in the Greek-speaking world. Thus the exact phrase occurs in Philo (*Aet. Mundi* 109) in reference to the four basic world elements of earth (γή), water (ὕδωρ), air (ἀήρ), and fire (πῦρ).[221] Paul apparently adds to this concept, however, when in vss. 8–9 he says that the Gentiles who formerly served beings who by nature were not gods are going back to the 'elements' (στοιχεῖα) by accepting the law. This makes it appear that the 'elements' are to be equated with pagan deities or the 'elemental spirits of the universe' as the *RSV* translates.[222] This presents a problem to many who argue that the word 'elements' did not refer to personal beings as such by the first century but developed this meaning only in later times.[223] They prefer to see in Paul's words the meaning of 'elementary teachings' or the like.

But this hesitation on the part of some may be unwarranted in the present context due to the fact that the Jews traditionally accused the Gentiles of worshipping the elements as gods (cf. Wisd. 13: 2; 7: 17; Philo *Vit. Com.* 3). Moreover, the phrase 'are not gods' (μὴ οὖσιν θεοῖς; Gal. 4: 8) obviously evokes a standard Jewish polemic against Gentile polytheistic worship.[224] This phrase in connection with 'the elements of the world' strongly suggests that although the word 'elements' (στοιχεῖα) may refer lexically at this time to the elements of the universe, Paul's reference is probably to these elements as they were worshipped by the Gentiles. If this is correct, it is not wrong to view these 'elements' as demonic elemental spirits.

But our primary concern in Gal. 4: 1–10 is not with the linguistic data that would or would not preclude the meaning of personal beings for 'elements' in the first century, since all the ingredients for this meaning were at least available long before Paul's time, but rather with the fact that this context appears to include both Judaism and paganism together under the servitude of the 'elements'. It is shocking to hear Paul say that the pagans who used to worship beings which were not truly gods, are *reverting back* to these 'elements' by accepting the law (vss. 8–9). Neil succinctly expresses the difficulty of the context when he says of vs. 3: 'It seems an astonishing thing to say, since he is obviously speaking of Jews as well as Gentiles.'[225]

Bligh attempts to explain the passage by arguing that Gal. 4: 1–10 belongs to the original Antioch discourse begun back in Gal. 2: 14 and refers to Jews only.[226] Paul begins Gal. 4 by saying:

> I mean that the heir, as long as he is a babe, is no better than a slave, though he is the owner of all the estate; but he is under guardians and trustees until the date set by the father. So with us: when we were children, we were slaves to the elemental spirits of the universe (Gal. 4: 1–3).

Bligh says that Paul cannot mean that before the coming of Christ the idolatrous pagans were sons and heirs, though treated as slaves. This applies only to Israel. In Gal. 4: 4–7 he argues that Paul speaks of the liberation of Israel only from the law: 'He cannot be speaking of the Gentiles here, since

they were not subject to the law of Moses.'[227] Also in vs. 8 when Paul
says that they were formerly enslaved to those beings which by nature are
not gods, Paul means that before the Jews were converted to Christ and
learned to cry Abba, Father, and had received the Holy Spirit, they were
enslaved to the angels of the law and had no direct communication from
God.[228]

Bligh does concede, however, that in a rough way these words could be
indirectly applied to the Galatians who before their conversion were in a
type of childhood and under demonic powers of paganism. Paul's words
could convey to the Galatians that Christ had redeemed them from the
sins which they had committed against the law of their consciences. But
in no way is the passage to be construed as relating directly to Gentiles or
to pagan religion. He says that the purpose of the passage is to point out
to Jewish Christians that their spiritual immaturity has ended and this
means that they must abandon their childhood practices which, among
other things, precludes a return to the law. 'In a word, the message is:
"You are now spiritual adults, and must behave as such." '[229]

A. J. Bandstra has a different approach to the text.[230] According to
him the first person plural pronoun used in Gal. 4: 1–5 refers to Jews; in
vs. 6b it refers to both Jews and Gentiles. He explains that this shift in the
reference of the pronoun presents a similar thought pattern to that of Gal.
3: 13–14. There he argues that Paul's meaning is that 'we' Jewish Christians
have been redeemed from the law so that the Gentiles might receive the
blessing of Abraham so that 'we' Jewish and Gentile Christians might
receive the promise of the Spirit. Thus in Gal. 4: 3–6 the meaning is that
at one time 'we' Jewish Christians were under the 'elements', but Christ
redeemed us from the law in order that 'we' Jewish Christians might
receive the adoption. And because 'you' Gentiles are sons, God sent the
Spirit of his son into 'our' (both Jewish and Gentile) hearts.[231] Gal. 4:
8–10, which contain the reference to the beings which are not gods, he
goes on to say, are addressed to Gentiles. In this way he avoids an
absolute equation of Judaism with paganism.

But while Bandstra does not make an absolute equation between Judaism and paganism he argues that there are some similarities. He notes that
each of the two appearances of the word 'elements' in Galatians is accompanied by a different adjectival reference, in Gal. 4: 3 by 'of the world'
($\tau o\tilde{v}$ $\kappa \acute{o}\sigma \mu o v$), in 4: 9 by 'weak and beggarly' ($\dot{a}\sigma \vartheta \epsilon v \tilde{\eta}$ $\kappa a\grave{\iota}$ $\pi \tau \omega \chi \acute{a}$). He says
that it is a fair assumption that the two mean the same thing. Taking one
of Paul's common meanings for the word 'world', and combining it with
the phrase 'weak and beggarly', he concludes that Paul has in mind 'those
elements that are operative within the whole sphere of human activity

which is temporary and passing away, beggarly and incompetent in bringing salvation, weak and both open to and defenseless before sin'.[232] These elements he identifies with the law and the flesh and argues that these had enslaved both the Jewish and Gentile worlds before and outside of Christ. Thus while Judaism and paganism were separate religious expressions, they both were plagued by these common forces and both needed redemption for their people.[233]

A more common approach, on the other hand, is to make no distinction at all in the pronouns but to see in them a common reference to both Jews and Gentiles. Thus Schlier comments on Gal. 4: 3: 'The "we" is thereby used absolutely unlimited in this connection and refers both to Jewish and Gentile Christians.'[234] Bo Reicke is a representative of this position.[235] He interprets the 'elements' as spiritual beings and argues that the angels through whom the law was given (Gal. 3: 19) are to be included among them. He says that the Jews, by being subject to the elemental spirits, actually worshipped beings which were not gods. He cites as evidence for this last statement, among other passages, 1 Cor. 10: 20 which he says is a reference to Jews who sacrifice to demons and not to God.[236] Furthermore, he argues that the law in cooperation with the flesh and its sinfulness at times seems to be more closely associated with this world than with its higher nature. Consequently, 'It is not unnatural for the law, as Paul actually conceived it, to be placed among the elemental spirits of the universe.'[237] Moreover, as the Jews were in servitude to the 'elements', along with the Gentiles, Reicke believes that the Gentiles were in servitude to the law, along with the Jews. They were under the law in the sense that they had the law of nature which to a certain extent is equivalent to the revelation the Jews received in the Torah. Paul can argue in Rom. 1: 18 – 3: 20 that all are guilty of breaking the demands of the law since the Gentiles through nature had access to the basic knowledge of God's law to the Jews. Thus Reicke argues that Gal. 4: 1–10 places Jews and Gentiles both under the elemental spirits of the universe and under the law, and that Christ's redemption is to be considered a redemption of both races.

A similar though not identical view is that of Caird.[238] He argues that Jesus did not come simply to offer redemption to those under the Torah. He offered redemption to all men under law because subservience to law is enslavement to the elemental spirits.[239] The key to Caird's position is his understanding of νόμος as 'law' rather than 'Torah', and since both Jews and Gentiles lived under law in some sense, both are included in Paul's meaning. He continues by relating Gal. 4: 8 specifically to the Gentiles who as former pagans worshipped beings which were not really gods. The problem is that Paul says they will revert back to these elemental spirits if they take on the burden of the law. This raises two questions for Caird: (1) If the elemental spirits are to be identified with pagan deities, how can the Galatians' acceptance of Jewish practices be said to be a lapse back to the elemental spirits? (2) What does Paul specifically mean by his notion that Gentiles live under law?

In answer to the first question Caird draws an analogy between pagan deities and the angels of the law. The pagan deities, according to him, were angelic beings to whom originally God delegated some authority, but who through idolatry had become exalted to a divine and absolute status. In a similar way the angelic mediators of the law had been made guardians of the Torah which Jewish orthodoxy had elevated to a supreme position. This means that both Jews and Gentiles were living under angelic regimes, both of which, though resting upon a divine institution, had distorted and frustrated the eternal purpose of God.[240]

In answer to the second question he says that the word νόμος could be used to mean the Jewish Torah or, in a wider Hellenistic sense, natural law. He believes that Paul uses it in both senses in the present passage. Both Jews and Gentiles are under the law in that the Jews are under the Torah and the Gentiles under natural law. By natural law the Gentiles have the ability to know God by the light of conscience. Caird then defines more carefully what natural law Paul had in mind. He says that it is that aspect of law which received impetus from the dissemination of astrology in the ancient world. In astrology the stars were held to be gods and were called 'the elements' (τὰ στοιχεῖα). These heavenly beings controlled the fates of men and held them in bonds of 'inexorable necessity'. The unalterable law of astrological fate came to rob men of hope and of meaning in life. Thus the appeal of Paul's preaching, according to Caird, to a large extent must have been in his offer of release from the bondage of the elemental spirits of the universe. Finally, he concludes: 'The demonic forces of legalism, then, both Jewish and Gentile, can be called "principalities and powers" or "elemental spirits of the world".'[241]

The interpretations of Reicke and Caird obviously differ in detail; nevertheless, they share in common the belief that both Jews and Gentiles before conversion were under the servitude of law. They argue this by using the word 'law' with different meanings, 'Torah' for the Jews, 'the law of nature' for the Gentiles, so that neither maintains that both Jews and Gentiles were *directly* and in the same way under the law of Moses.[242] In fact a great many interpreters, with only minor variations and regardless of whether they understand 'elements' as personal beings or elementary teachings, believe that in some sense Paul's words in these verses pertain both to Jews and Gentiles in that both were in bondage to law.

Burton, for example, who believes that 'the elements of the world' are 'the rudimentary religious teachings possessed by the race', says that Christ redeemed both Jew and Gentile from the bondage of law since both were enslaved to legalistic principles.[243] Likewise, Neil, who, on the other hand, believes that the 'elements' are spiritual beings, describes the plight of Jews and Gentiles as bondage to legalism: 'What Paul means is that both paganism and Judaism are religions which make men slaves. They are subject to external compulsion, they live in fear of inadvertently doing something wrong, they are helpless victims of an arbitrary power.'[244] Indeed it may be said that a distinctive characteristic of the word 'law' in the history of the interpretation of this passage is the concept of enslavement to legalism. This concept is used to explain Paul's apparent equation between Judaism and paganism. Since both are legal systems, to be under one is tantamount to being under the other and to be under either is to be under the 'elements'.

Another approach to Paul's apparent equation of Judaism with paganism, which many place alongside 'legalism' as a common element between them, is that Judaism and paganism served as preparatory training to the world before the advent of Christ. Lightfoot, for example, says: 'Judaism was a system of bondage like Heathenism. Heathenism had been a disciplinary training like Judaism.'[245] Apparently the meaning behind this view is that the period of training under law was preparation for the advent of Christ. Law taught man his inability to attain salvation on his own merit. It taught him the need for salvation from God by grace. Law underscored sin and even increased it. In this sense, then, both Judaism with its Torah and paganism with its law converged and formed a disciplinary period in which the human race was prepared for the coming of Christianity. Though these religious systems were preparatory for Christ, and in this sense they rendered a positive service to mankind, neither was effectual in bringing about salvation since all were under the weak and beggarly elements (Gal. 4: 9). Thus Leivestad, who believes that both the law and the 'elements' had a positive function to perform, says: 'But with regard to the salvation of man both are weak and ineffective, they are even obstacles that must be cleared away.'[246] Burton contrasts the old religions with the power and richness of the gospel and says that paganism and Judaism 'were at bottom legalistic, without clear perception of ethical principles and destitute of dynamic to make possible the realisation of them in life'.[247]

II

More could be said about the history of the interpretation of Gal. 4: 1–10. The positions sampled above are sufficient to point out certain common problems. One of the most crucial lies in the area of semantics. A number of words are used which lend themselves to more than one definition. The word 'law', for instance, serves to formulate a parallelism between Judaism and paganism even though it is used with more than one meaning. The word 'bondage' is used correlatively with 'law', often without an explanation of how the two are related. This problem will have to be aired more fully later. For the moment it is to be noted that Paul's apparent equation between Judaism and paganism is generally explained in terms of similarities between them, that is, both were in bondage to legalism. But few explain Paul's equation in terms of actual identity. Few argue that Paul actually considered the Gentiles to be under the Torah.[248] Nor do many describe Judaism as paganistic.[249] Most interpreters simply draw parallels between the two, often in a limited sense, and thus attempt to satisfy Paul's language.

This last point is significant. Lightfoot, for example, is careful to distinguish between that part of paganism which is like the Torah and that part which is not. He says that both paganism and Judaism are made up of two aspects: (1) the spiritual, and (2) the ritualistic. As to their spiritual aspects the two are worlds apart. Paganism is diabolical; Judaism is divine. But when Christ came the law's spiritual qualities were absorbed into the new Christian religion and that left the law a mass of lifeless ordinances, deprived of its spiritual aspects. According to him only the ritualistic aspects of Judaism which were left converged with paganism. 'They had at least this in common, that as ritual systems they were made up of precepts and ordinances, and thus were representatives of "law" as opposed to "grace", "promise", that is, as opposed to the Gospel.'[250] Thus Lightfoot parallels Judaism and paganism in a limited way. They have only the common element of ritual between them and otherwise are quite different.

But it is questionable that Paul intended to make a limited parallelism between Judaism and paganism in the present passage. He makes no clear distinction between those parts of the law which are objectionable and those which are not.[251] In Gal. 4: 10 he says that the Galatians are observing days, months, seasons, and years, but this is not an enumeration of only those parts of the law which he considers offensive. Circumcision, which Paul obviously has in mind as a prime target throughout the letter, is not mentioned. Gal. 4: 10 rather appears to be an expression of disappointment at the readers' acceptance of the Torah as a whole.

To rescue Paul from equating paganism and Judaism by arguing that ritual is *the* point of commonality between them is an effort which fails to consider all the evidence. Paul never objects to paganism on the grounds of ritualism. He objects to it because it is idolatrous and immoral; it suppresses the truth about God and leads men to worship demons (cf. Rom. 1:

18-32; 1 Cor. 10: 20-21). In view of this it is unlikely that any formula-
tion of a limited parallel between Judaism and paganism, that is based on
the notion of ritualism or legalism, will successfully correspond to Paul's
real view of paganism. Ragner Bring refers to Gal. 4: 10 as the key to the
problem. To him, Paul's reference to the calendrical religious observances
of the Galatians means that the element of legalism is the common characteristic of Judaism and paganism to which Paul objects. He says:

> He picks out characteristics which are common to both the earlier
> heathen cult of the Galatians and Judaism. He has in mind that
> attitude in and through which man seeks to protect and save him-
> self from the influence of dangerous powers and seeks to find for
> himself a safe way by propitiating the 'powers', or by living in the
> observance of the law.[252]

But where does Paul ever criticize paganism for fostering an attitude
which leads man to protect and save himself from the influence of danger-
ous powers or which causes him to seek a safe way by propitiating the
powers or by living in observance of the law? Paul's description of paganism is radically different from this. He says that the Gentiles 'exchanged
the glory of the incorruptible God for the likeness of images of corruptible
man and of birds and of four-footed beasts and of reptiles' (Rom. 1: 22-3).
He says that God gave them up in the lust of their hearts 'because they
exchanged the truth of God for a lie and worshipped and served the crea-
ture rather than the creator' (Rom. 1: 24-5). The emphasis in these statements is not on the fact that the Gentiles 'worshipped' and 'served', but
on the fact that they worshipped and served *idols*. Paul's objection to
Gentile religion is that it is the worship of idols. The evils of paganism with
Paul can hardly be summarized by the words 'ritualism' or 'legalism'.

Caird realizes this and attempts to base, at least partially, the similarity
between Judaism and Heathenism on the concept of idolatry. As we have
seen, he says that the pagan gods, in the Jewish belief, were angelic beings
who had received a measure of God's own authority, but whose original
character, through idolatrous worship, had become corrupted and exalted
to a position of absolute divine status. He says that in Paul's mind the
angelic mediators of the law occupied an analogous position in that they
had been made guardians of the Torah which Jewish orthodoxy had elevated to a supreme position. Thus both Jews and Gentiles were living under
angelic regimes which distorted and frustrated the eternal purpose of
God.[253]

But a close look at this analogy reveals two immediate problems. First
it has the angelic beings of paganism exalted to the place of a divine and

absolute status, while it is the Torah which it says Jewish orthodoxy elevated, not the angelic beings which mediated it. For the analogy to be appropriate it would have to be the angels of the Torah which Jewish orthodoxy elevated to an absolute status, not the Torah. Second, it fails to make clear how the Torah in any sense is parallel to idolatry. The Old Testament taught and Judaism accepted absolute obedience to the Torah as a means to combat idolatry. To Jewish orthodoxy the Torah was the revelation of the one true God which they worshipped. Thus, it is unclear at what point the Torah and idolatry become parallel.

Caird continues his analogy between Judaism and paganism in terms of 'law'. He says that Paul used the word νόμος both in reference to the Torah and in reference to the law of nature. The concept of 'natural law' may refer to the idea of receiving divine revelation and enlightenment through nature.[254] Obviously Caird at first has this in mind when he says: 'He argues that the Gentiles have the capacity to know God, though few in fact have chosen to exercise it. He is prepared to admit that among the Gentiles there are men living, by the light of conscience, lives which compare favourably with the lives of most Jews.'[255] But then suddenly and quite unexpectedly he shifts over to the concept of law in astrology:

> In astrology the heavenly bodies were regarded as divine beings and known as τὰ στοιχεῖα; under the influence of their regular motions the whole of human life was controlled by bonds of inexorable necessity... The iron rule of an impersonal fate robbed life both of meaning and of hope, and no small part of the appeal of Paul's preaching must have been that it offered release from servitude to the elemental spirits.[256]

This shift from 'natural law' to the 'iron rule of an impersonal fate' is confusing. In the first place there may be a concept of natural law in Paul which is parallel to the Torah, in that like the Torah, nature reveals to man the universality of the one true God (Rom. 1 and 2). Paul held that those who observe nature closely could see through the fallacy of idolatry and could conceivably keep themselves from it. Conversely, those who are idolaters are 'without excuse' since the true nature of God is clearly seen in the things that are made (Rom. 1: 18–23). But the shift from natural law in this sense to law in astrology breaks off any real similarity between law and the Torah. The Torah could hardly be called an 'iron rule of an impersonal fate' which robbed life of meaning and hope. It did not control 'the whole of human life... by bonds of inexorable necessity'.

When Caird himself describes the Torah it is in vastly different terms from this. For him the Torah is a legal system which demanded actions on the part of men. It leads men to commit the sin of pride. 'All legalism is self-assertion, a claim that we can establish our own righteousness, that we can save ourselves by our own moral and spiritual attainments; and such a claim makes it impossible for us to know God in his true nature as the God of grace.' [257] But this is unlike the law of fate which was operative in astrology. Fate required nothing of anyone. It merely gripped men in the bonds of destiny and placed a seal upon the happenings of life.[258] There could be no self-assertion or claims of righteousness in astrology. No one could boast of saving himself by his moral and spiritual attainments in obedience to impersonal fate.

This discussion of the law and its relationship with paganism apparently rests upon two somewhat unrelated assumptions. First, it rests upon the assumption that to be subject to the requirements of law is to be under bondage. In Galatians in particular Paul uses the concept of 'bondage' to form one of his strongest arguments against the law (see Gal. 4: 21 – 5: 1). For the Galatians to accept the Torah, in Paul's mind, was for them to submit to bondage. This idea is usually understood to mean that subservience to legal requirements is an evil which enslaves men. The second assumption is that legalism leads to the sin of pride. It is self-assertive and self-righteous.

But can these two assumptions be maintained? In regard to the latter, law-keeping, from one point of view, is the very opposite. It implies subservience to a higher power and is actually a denial of one's self-sufficiency. The law-keeper sacrifices to God in order to please him, begs for mercy when he sins, and in general places himself at God's disposal. Such actions can hardly be considered as proud and self-assertive. They are better described as actions of deep humility. In regard to the former, it is doubtful that 'bondage' is strictly applicable to a system whose characteristic ingredient is a set of legal requirements.[259] It is generally assumed that legal requirements automatically place one in bondage. But this is not necessarily true. No one in the Free World can legitimately say that civil law enslaves man. In one sense our law is what keeps us free. Moreover, man is always at liberty to rebel against law whenever he likes as history so clearly shows. In this respect God's law is no different. No one is bound to keep God's law in the absolute sense. Proof of this is found in the multitude of biblical exhortations for man to be obedient to God's law. Such language is hardly in keeping with the concept of law as a bondage from which there is no escape. The fact is, man's problem never has been his enslavement to God's requirements; often, as Scripture shows, his problem has been estrangement from them.

As regards the Galatians, it is clear that prior to conversion their problem was not that they were struggling under a law that was too hard to keep or that they were proud of their accomplishments. Their problem was that they were enslaved to evil spirits who darkened their minds and led them into idolatry. They were ignorant of God and hopelessly lost in the clutches of paganism. In no sense does this correspond to the modern notions of enslavement to law and the pride which comes from the performance of law. Therefore, when Paul warns the Galatians of the danger of becoming enslaved again to their former captors by accepting the law, he must imply that they are in danger of something other than legalism.

As for the concept of boasting, Paul does speak of it, but he does so in a way that is unrelated to the modern concept of pride. In Rom. 3: 27-30 he says that boasting has been excluded by a law of faith. But he goes on to say that this is because God is the God of both Jews and Gentiles.[260] Paul objects to boasting because it implies that God is the God of the Jews only. In Rom. 10: 3-4 he says that the Jews seek to establish their own righteousness and do not subject themselves to the righteousness of God. He clarifies this by explaining that Christ is the end of the law *to everyone who believes*.[261] This leads him into an exposition of the universality of the gospel, as his concluding remarks to this section show (Rom. 10: 12-13). Thus it is clear that 'boasting' and the attempt to establish one's own righteousness, in the sense that Paul uses these terms, are related to his doctrine of the inclusion of the Gentiles. Boasting, to the Christian, is excluded because all men are included.

All of this shows a need to rethink Paul's language about the law. In the next section we will attempt to show that the key to his thinking is his understanding of the universality of the gospel.

III

To understand Paul's equation of Judaism with paganism in Gal. 4: 1-10 it is important to begin with the distinguishing characteristics of paganism and relate them to Judaism rather than vice versa. As we have seen, many interpreters start in the opposite direction. They begin with the Torah explaining its problem in terms of legalism; then they parallel this with ritualism in paganism. Finally they conclude that the Galatians, by accepting the legalistic requirements of the Torah, are placing themselves in the same position they were in before their conversion, namely, in bondage to legal requirements. We have already noted the problems connected with this kind of parallelism and need not be concerned with it further.

It is much more in line with Paul's own procedure to begin with paganism and to understand the Galatians' acceptance of the Torah as a return to the elemental spirits of the universe. In other words, Paul's point is that

the Galatians, by accepting the law, are returning to idolatry. This seems
to be his meaning in the following passage:

> But at one time, when you did not know God, you were enslaved
> to those beings which by nature are not gods. But now, since you
> have come to know God, or rather to be known by God, how can
> you turn again to the weak and beggarly elemental spirits, to which
> again once more you wish to be enslaved (Gal. 4: 8–9).

We have seen that some attempt to equate Judaism with idolatry.
Reicke, for instance, says that the mediating angels of the law, mentioned
in Gal. 3: 19, are to be placed among the elemental spirits so that an
acceptance of the law is for the Galatians a return to their old system.
But there are reasons to argue against this interpretation. Elsewhere, the
angelic mediatorship of the law lacks the negative connotations Reicke
places upon it.[262] Even in Gal. 3: 19 the negative implications are minimal.
There Paul's argument is not that the law is inferior to the promise because
it was delivered by angels, but rather that the law is *separate* from the promise. The function of Paul's reference to the angels of the law is to distinguish and isolate the law from the promise, not to depreciate it.

Paul's equation of Judaism with paganism is much better viewed from
a different angle. The issue which Paul faced in the Gentile world was
polytheism and it is from this point of view that his analogy between the
law and the old religion of the Galatians must be understood. Polytheism
in the ancient world was the belief in local deities, which fostered the
corresponding concept of diversity in humanity.[263] In Hellenistic and
Roman times the old religions experienced a rapid process of syncretism,
but still the basic concept of disunity in the world of gods and men pre-
vailed, exerting itself in new forms.[264]

It is noteworthy that Intertestamental Judaism, though its literature was
written during this time of syncretism, continued to look upon the gods of
the nations in much the same way that the Old Testament prophets did. It
taught that Gentile religion was the worship of demon-gods who served
as the rulers of the nations.[265] It predicted that an age would come when
there would be an end to this falsehood and when truth would be established (cf. *IQS* iv. 18–23). All nations at that time would leave their idols
and come to the God of Abraham in united peace (cf. 1 Enoch 90: 28–42
and Isa. 2: 2–3).

Paul's point of view is most certainly that of the Intertestamental period.
He viewed the pagan gods as demons (1 Cor. 10: 20) who held the Gentile
world in the bondage of idolatry. They had blinded the eyes of men so
that they were ignorant of the true God and the concept of universal

humanity. As a Christian Paul also believed that Christ had destroyed this deceit through his resurrection so that man was no longer held captive in this bondage.[266] It is this point of view toward Gentile religion that gives meaning to Paul's reference to the Galatians' return *via* the law to the elemental spirits. The particular aspect of the law which Paul had in mind is its power to divide Jew from Gentile. We pointed out in the last chapter that the law suppressed all men in pre-Christian times by separating Jews from Gentiles. Then Christ came and kept faith with the promise to Abraham that all nations would be blessed and the law lost its pedagogical status. Through faith all became sons of God whether Jew, Greek, bond, free, male, or female (Gal. 3: 22-9).

Nevertheless, Paul was alarmed at the situation which had developed in Galatia, for although his gospel had changed the Galatians from polytheists into monotheists, the judaizers were preaching a message which would change them back into polytheists. The imposition of the requirements of the Torah upon Gentiles served to change the universal nature of Yahweh into that of a national god. For the judaizers to insist that the Gentiles could not be saved without becoming Jewish proselytes, in Paul's mind, was the same as turning Christianity into a local cult. There could be no belief in Yahweh as the one God of the universe as long as the church presented him as the God of Israel only. Until the church admitted uncircumcised Gentiles into the kingdom, strictly on the basis of their faith in Yahweh, Paul knew that the universal nature of God would remain suppressed.

This is why Paul is so adamant in his letter. For the Galatians to accept circumcision was for them to return to the concept of local deities and to be enslaved once again to the elemental spirits of the universe. It was for them to lose that feature of Christianity which for Paul was its distinguishing mark, namely, belief in one God who is the Father of all men. Disruption either in the notion of one God or of one humanity, in his mind, would automatically destroy the whole concept of universality which was the major ingredient of Christianity presented by his gospel. Nor must it be thought that his concern with God's universal nature was only for the sake of the Gentiles. So long as the Jews demanded circumcision of the Gentiles they too fell short of the correct understanding of God. It was as important for the Jews to accept uncircumcised Gentiles as it was for the Gentiles to refuse the law. Paul knew that so long as the law was required of Gentiles neither side would be free from the suppression of the elemental spirits.

It may be that Paul's silence over James' possible culpableness in the Antioch incident has relevance at this point. It is notable that he says that

Peter withdrew from the Gentiles after men came from James (Gal. 2: 12); but in his indictment he accuses Peter, Barnabas and the rest of the Jews, but not James. It seems unreasonable to think that if James had been the instigator of Peter's withdrawal from the Gentiles and his attempt to compel them to be circumcised that Paul would have passed over his faults in total silence. In fact his treatment of James is so neutral that some have conjectured that 'certain ones from James' refers only to those who had come from the circle of James' influence, or the like, and not to special messengers sent out by James himself.[267]

Though we may never know the answer to Paul's silence, it may be conjectured that James understood Paul's gospel better than Peter and in fact was closer to Paul in theology than Peter.[268] He, like Paul, may have understood that for Yahweh to be the God of all men the Jews had to accept the Gentiles as they were, uncircumcised, and the Gentiles had to accept the Jews as they were, circumcised. The acceptance of Torah-abiding Jews by the Gentiles was as important for Paul's universal gospel as the acceptance of non-Torah-abiding Gentiles by the Jews.

Paul's gospel was deeply rooted in the belief that Yahweh, the God of Abraham, was the God of the Gentiles. The unity which Paul envisioned corresponded to this; it was a unity between Jews and Gentiles. This is certainly his point of view in Rom. 3: 29–30 where he says: 'Or is God the God of the Jews only? Is he not the God of the Gentiles also? Yes, of the Gentiles also, since God is one.' His thought is: if God is one he must be the God of both Jews and Gentiles. Belief in Yahweh as the one universal God thus demanded mutual recognition between Jews and Gentiles that they both belonged to the same God. We may even go further and say that any attempt on either side to erase the ethnic and cultural nature of the other would be to destroy Paul's particular concept of unity between Jews and Gentiles. The effort of Jewish Christians to force Gentiles to accept circumcision and the law was just such an attempt and Paul saw immediately that it tended to make Yahweh into a national God, the God of the Jews only. On the other hand, the repudiation of circumcision and the law by the Jews would break Christianity loose from the Hebrew tradition which was important for it in Paul's view of things and would change its teachings on unity into a Stoic-type concept of world-citizenship. There was something inherent within Paul's gospel that especially stood against this latter. Paul's concept of unity was not simply unity among men, viz., a world-citizenship, but unity between Israel and the nations. His concept was based on the Hebrew tradition[269] that the God of Abraham was working in history to overcome the pagan gods of the nations so that eventually he would be acknowledged as the God of all men. In Romans 11 Paul

describes God as maneuvering Israel and the nations in such a way as eventually to include all within his kingdom (cf. Rom. 11: 11–36). Thus it is
necessary for Paul's thought to distinguish ethnically between Jews and
Gentiles since each had an ethnic role to play in the salvation of the
other.[270] The ultimate goal, in Paul's mind, was the mutual recognition
of each under the divine rule of Yahweh, the God of Abraham.

It is possible, as we have said, that James' understanding of this at the
Jerusalem meeting, described in Gal. 2: 1–10, was more perceptive than
Peter's. Those who came to Antioch from James may have cautioned Peter
only not to Hellenize completely and thus destroy the ethnic distinctiveness between Jews and Gentiles. Peter, on the other hand, may have failed
to perceive this distinction which James was making and concluded that
the law was necessary not only for him but for the Gentiles as well. At
any rate he was completely wrong about the matter and was summarily
rebuked by Paul. The gospel as Paul preached it could not exist under
such terms.

It is noteworthy that from the perspective presented here many of the
conflicts between Acts and Paul's letters are mitigated. It may be, for
instance, that James' insistence on the prescriptions in the Apostolic
Decree of Acts 15 does not reflect an ultra-conservative position on his
part due to his inability to grasp fully Paul's gospel.[271] It is just as reasonable to suppose that his actions were solely to facilitate unity between the
Jewish and Gentile wings of the church. In his mind table-fellowship with
the Gentiles may not in any way have involved an infraction of the law,
though it apparently did for a certain Pharisaical element within the Jewish
church. The Gentiles, by complying with the Noachian laws of the Apostolic Decree, could thereby bridge the gap between the two without
destroying the ethnic distinctions of either group.

Again, judging from Acts 15 and 21 (which is perhaps the clearest passage in the New Testament on the continued observance of the law by the
Jerusalem church), it appears that Paul and James are in agreement. It has
often been thought that Acts 21 is so far removed from Paul's gospel that
it cannot be historical. For Paul to enter the Temple in order to make a
sacrifice seems beyond the realm of possibility for the Paul of the Epistles.
Moreover, the submissiveness of Paul to James and the Jerusalem church
as presented in Acts is in conflict with the traditional interpretation of
Galatians 1 and 2. But we have seen that the traditional interpretation of
Galatians 1 and 2 is highly problematic. From all appearances Paul's one
and only concern in regard to the matter of 'independence' was the independence of his non-circumcision gospel to the Gentiles. In all probability
Paul was disinterested in church polity and could not have cared less

whether he or James or someone else was the 'top man'.

Moreover, Paul's particular insistence on unity between Jews and Gentiles, as opposed to some nebulous concept of world unity, gives the continued observance of the law on the part of Jewish Christianity an important role to play within his gospel. Due to the nature of things, viz., the pressure of judaizers to circumcise Gentiles, most of Paul's insistence in this matter consists of denials of such demands. In fact his position is that the Gentiles will be damned if they accept circumcision (Gal. 5: 2–4). But under other circumstances he might have insisted on the importance of Israel's retention of her distinctiveness. The eleventh chapter of Romans, in particular, presents God's salvific plan for all men as incorporating the ethnic and cultural distinctiveness of both Jews and Gentiles.

All of this is to say that with Paul salvation is the unification of uncircumcised, non-Torah-abiding Gentiles with circumcised, Torah-abiding Jews under the one divine headship of Yahweh, the God of Abraham. This does not mean that Paul envisioned two gospels, one for the Jews and one for the Gentiles. It rather suggests that the one gospel which he received by revelation from Jesus Christ consisted of the unification of these two distinct groups of people, Jews and Gentiles. Any action on the part of one to erase the ethnic nature of the other would constitute an automatic eradication of his gospel. This is not to say that observance of the law for the Jewish Christian was necessary for his individual salvation. In other words, Paul would never say that a Jew had to be circumcised to be saved. Such notions were beyond his realm of thought. With Paul all men are saved alike by the grace of God. On the other hand, Paul would say that observance of the law by Jewish Christianity was important for the salvation of the Gentile world and that non-observance of the law by Gentile Christians was important for the salvation of the Jewish world. Only in this way could he proclaim Yahweh, the God of the Hebrews, as the God of all nations. Only in this way could Israel ever conceptualize *their* God as a universal God, and only in this way could the Gentiles conceptualize the one God of the world as *the God of Abraham the Hebrew*. Any other arrangement would place the gospel into the realm of pagan philosophy or religion.

The presence of judaizers in Galatia in this sense was thus ominous. If left unchecked, it would destroy the foundations of the gospel of Christ. Paul had faced judaizers earlier, and had even been to Jerusalem before the 'pillars' to set forth the gospel he preached with its implications for unity. To his delight he saw them extend their right hands in fellowship in recognition of his Gentile apostleship. But his joy was short-lived for at Antioch Peter wavered. The full magnitude of the gospel was hard for him

to grasp. Now new judaizers were in Galatia attempting to turn the gospel
of one God into a national cult. The reason Paul equated their work with
polytheism is because it was polytheism. Unless fellowship was maintained
between Jews (as Jews) and Gentiles (as Gentiles) neither branch of the
church would be truly monotheistic. They would be forever suppressed by
the law and forced to serve the demonic powers. Until the partitioning
effects of the law were removed the 'elements of the universe' would be
their masters.

This was the danger of which Paul warned the Galatians. His alarm at
their acceptance of circumcision was not that in submitting to the law they
were submitting to legalism and thus losing their freedom. Legalism to him
was not the monster it is to modern theology. His alarm was at the Galatians' return to the demonic powers in the universe. These powers, which
in the past had held them in inexorable chains, were not to be served again.
The God that Paul preached was the God of all men and this meant that all
men must accept him on universal terms. The faith of the Gentiles in Yahweh was all that was needed to make them one body with the Jews in Christ.

Again we see that the key to Paul's thought in Galatians is his doctrine
of the inclusion of uncircumcised Gentiles. His understanding of the universal gospel was obviously greater than that of Peter. Peter perhaps at first
saw it, but, at least temporarily, lost it. Barnabas, Paul's companion, saw it,
but fell away with Cephas. Paul the apostle to the Gentiles fully grasped it.
From the moment Christ revealed it to him he held in his power the unity
of the church and with it belief in one God. In retrospect he stands as a
giant. Having to wait as he did to reveal the truth to the 'pillars', he no
doubt subjected himself to untold suffering. At Antioch he stood alone as
all deserted with Peter. In Galatia he bravely faced a critical moment in
time when the universal gospel hung in the balance. History shows that the
scales tipped in Paul's favor and that the church accepted the implications
of one God. From these shaky beginnings Paul the apostle to the Gentiles
shaped the church into the great unity it came to be, one body made up
of all nations.

NOTES

1   For two recent studies on Baur see W. Geiger, *Spekulation und Kritik:
    Die Geschichtstheologie Ferdinand Christian Baurs*, and P. C. Hodgson,
    The Formation of Historical Theology.
2   Baur, *Tübinger Zeitschrift für Theologie*, V: 4 (1831), 61–206.
3   For an excellent survey of Jewish Christian studies from Baur to the
    present see A. F. J. Klijn, 'The Study of Jewish Christianity', *NTS* 20
    (1974), 419–31. Also helpful is C. K. Barrett, 'Pauline Controversies in
    the Post-Pauline Period', *NTS*, 20 (1974), 229–45.
4   F. C. Baur, *Paulus, der Apostel Jesu Christi. Sein Leben und Wirken, seine
    Briefe und seine Lehre. Ein Beitrag zu einer kritischen Geschichte des
    Urchristenthums.* An English translation of the 2nd edition in two volumes
    by E. Zeller (cited in the present work) is *Paul the Apostle of Jesus Christ,
    His Life and Work, His Epistles and His Doctrine. A Contribution to a
    Critical History of Primitive Christianity.*
5   Baur, *Paul*, I, 121.
6   Klijn, The Study of Jewish Christianity', 420.
7   For an excellent survey of early disciples as well as opponents of Baur see
    W. G. Kümmel, *The New Testament: The History of the Investigation of
    Its Problems*, 144–84.
8   J. B. Lightfoot, *St Paul's Epistle to the Galatians.* I have had access only
    to the sixth edition of 1880.
9   *Ibid.*, 371f.
10 H. J. Schoeps, *Paulus: Die Theologie des Apostels im Lichte der jüdischen
    Religionsgeschichte.* The English translation in revised form (quoted here)
    is *Paul: The Theology of the Apostle in the Light of Jewish Religious
    History.*
11 *Ibid.*, 69.
12 R. Jewett, 'The Agitators and the Galatian Congregation', *NTS*, 17 (1970–
    71), 198–212. See also R. Jewett, *Paul's Anthropological Terms. A Study
    of Their Use in Conflict Settings*, 17–20.
13 Jewett, 'The Agitators and the Galatian Congregation', 205.
14 *Ibid.*, 207.
16 W. Lütgert, *Gesetz und Geist: eine Untersuchung zur Vorgeschichte des
    Galaterbriefes.*
17 J. H. Ropes, *The Singular Problem of the Epistle to the Galatians*, 23.
18 F. R. Crownfield, 'The Singular Problem of the Dual Galatians', *JBL*, 63
    (1945), 491–500.

19 *Ibid.*, 493.
20 J. Munck, *Paulus und die Heilsgeschichte*. The English translation (quoted here) is *Paul and the Salvation of Mankind*.
21 *Ibid.*, 276.
22 *Ibid.*, 89. M. Barth supports Munck's thesis in 'The Kerygma of Galatians', *Interpretation*, 21 (1967), 131–46. See the earlier work of E. Hirsch, 'Zwei Fragen zu Galater 6, *ZNW*, 29 (1930), 192–7, who holds a similar view, and cf. O. Holtzmann, 'Zu Emanuel Hirsch, Zwei Fragen zu Galater 6, *ZNW*, 30 (1931), 76–83.
23 *ZNW*, 47 (1956), 25–67.
24 W. Schmithals, 'Die Häretiker in Galatien', *Paulus und die Gnostiker*. The English translation (quoted here) is *Paul & the Gnostics*.
25 *Ibid.*, 19.
26 *Ibid.*, 25.
27 Baur, *Paul*, I, 253.
28 Ropes, *Singular Problem*, 12.
29 Schoeps, *Paul*, 78.
30 See J. B. Tyson, 'Paul's Opponents in Galatia', *NT*, 10 (1968), 241–54, who works out an elaborate method for identifying the opponents from the implications of the charges.
31 Ropes, *Singular Problem*, 21.
32 Schmithals, *Paul & the Gnostics*, 23.
33 J. Bligh, *Galatians: A Discussion of St Paul's Epistle*, 33.
34 Ropes, *Singular Problem*, 21–2.
35 Munck, *Paul and the Salvation of Mankind*, 90. See also O. Bauernfeind, 'Die Begegnung zwischen Paulus und Kephas, Gal. 1: 18–20', *ZNW*, 47 (1956), 268–76, who says that the opponents charged Paul with hiding from the Galatians the seriousness of keeping the law so as not to lose his converts. Likewise R. Bring, *Commentary on Galatians*, 55, explains the charge: 'But in order to please men Paul had delivered only a part of the message, leaving out that which might have been difficult for the Gentiles to accept.'
36 Schmithals, *Paul & the Gnostics*, 58, relates this charge to 1 Thess. 2: 4 with the apparent meaning that Paul pleases the community in order to enrich himself with the collection.
37 Jewett, 'The Agitators and the Galatian Congregation', 206.
38 If N. J. McEleney is right in his belief that Diaspora Judaism was less insistent on circumcision for proselytes than Palestinian Judaism, his con- clusion is possibly an argument in favor of the view that the agitators in Galatia were of Palestinian extraction, given their insistence on circum- cision. See N. J. McEleney, 'Conversion, Circumcision and the Law', *NTS*, 20 (1974), 323.
39 W. M. Ramsay, *The Church in the Roman Empire*, 59–68; D. J. Selby, *Toward the Understanding of St. Paul*, 145–8.
40 J. J. Gunther, *St. Paul's Opponents and Their Background: A Study of Apocalyptic and Jewish Sectarian Teachings*, 10.
41 Baur, *Paul*, I, 255.
42 Bligh, *Galatians: A Discussion of St Paul's Epistle*, 436.
43 Ropes, *Singular Problem*, 23.

44 Schmithals, *Paul & the Gnostics*, 55.
45 Jewett, 'The Agitators and the Galatian Congregation', 212.
46 I doubt Jewett's thesis that 'flesh' applies to the nomists in that they trust in what their own flesh can accomplish, and to antinomists, in that in their libertine morality they seek life (viz., 'the sexual objects calling forth πορνεία, ἀκαθαρσία and ἀσέλγεια offer man a moment of intense life, psychological security and a way to reduce the sexual partner to submission') *Paul's Anthropological Terms*, 95–105, especially 104.
47 On this point see especially A. J. Bandstra, *The Law and the Elements of the World. An Exegetical Study in Aspects of Paul's Teaching*, 109–10, 131–3. Also see B. Reicke, 'The Law and this World According to Paul: Some Thoughts concerning Gal 4: 1–11', *JBL*, 70 (1951), 267, where the author says: 'Thus we find a certain tendency to associate the ideas Law and flesh until these terms become almost synonymous.' J. B. Tyson, ' "Works of Law" in Galatians', *JBL*, 92 (1973), 429, denies that the works of the flesh in Gal. 5: 19 have anything to do with the works of the law. This is remarkable in light of the fact that earlier (p. 427) he places 'flesh' and 'works of law' together against 'believing acceptance' and 'the spirit'.
48 Jewett, *Paul's Anthropological Terms*, 145–6 says: 'So the argument in 7: 7–12 [Romans] is that ἐπιθυμία was the desire aroused by the law to justify oneself by works.' We find this unacceptable and non-Pauline. In our judgment, K. Stendahl, 'The Apostle Paul and the Introspective Conscience of the West', *HTR*, 56 (1963), 199–215, is an indirect refutation of the whole thrust of Jewett's argument. Particularly applicable is: 'We should venture to suggest that the West for centuries has wrongly surmised that the biblical writers were grappling with problems which no doubt are ours, but which never entered their consciousness' (p. 214). We shall attempt to show in Chapters 3 and 4 that Paul's problem with the law was concerned not with the meritorious works of man which it supposedly aroused, but with the inclusion of the Gentiles. In Chapter 3 we argue that the Jewish Christians continued to keep the law. This seems to create a conflict in Paul's thought as presented above. If to be under the law is to be in the flesh, how could Jewish Christianity continue to keep the law? The answer given in Chapter 3 is that only those who were under the divisive effects of the law (i.e., those effects which separated Jew from Gentile) were under it in a fleshly way. In the ethical section of Galatians it is this aspect of the law which we conceive as Paul's concern. The point is: 'If you Gentile Galatians accept the law, you are saying that only Jews can be saved. This discrimination against the ethnic distinctiveness of the Gentiles brings on enslavement to the flesh.'
49 Crownfield, 'The Singular Problem of the Dual Galatians', 500.
50 Schmithals, *Paul & the Gnostics*, 33.
51 Lightfoot, *Galatians*, 222.
52 Bligh, *Galatians: A Discussion of St Paul's Epistle*, 32.
53 Jewett, 'The Agitators and the Galatian Congregation', 205–7. Jewett's thesis is plausible as an explanation for a judaizing campaign among the Gentile Christians in Judea (if indeed they were not already circumcised) since it would be difficult to disassociate the church from them there. To circumcise them would possibly make the best out of a bad situation. But

it is questionable that the Judean churches would have conceived of a judaizing program in Asia Minor in the same way. To go out of the country for such purposes at that particular time would have served to draw attention to the church's preoccupation with Gentiles in heathen lands. It is hard to see how this would have relieved pressure from the Jews because of their association with Gentiles. Jewett further notes that 1 Thess. 2: 14–16 alludes to an antichristian persecution in Judea during this time. It is interesting to note as well that here Paul says that the Jews hinder him from speaking to the Gentiles that they might be saved. There is no mention that it would be all right if he circumcised them.

54 R. McL. Wilson, 'Gnostics – in Galatia?', *SE*, 4 (1968), 361. (= *TU* no. 102, 1968).

55 Cf. our interpretation, *infra*, Chapter 3.

56 Cf. the synonymous phrases: God created the world/God created the *whole* world. The difference between them is one of emphasis, not substance. One who is a 'debtor' to do the *whole* law is in absolute slavery. There is no one to share his indebtedness. Paul points to the severity of the slavery that the Galatians' actions threaten to bring.

57 Munck, *Paul and the Salvation of Mankind*, 87.

58 C. H. Talbert, 'Again: Paul's Visits to Jerusalem', *NT*, 9 (1967), 27–8.

59 Munck, *Paul and the Salvation of Mankind*, 89.

60 Lightfoot, *Galatians*, 222.

61 J. Bligh, *Galatians in Greek*, 218. Jewett argues that Paul could not use the past form of the participle as some manuscripts do (possibly to correct false notions of the present; i.e., περιτετμημένοι, P⁴⁶, B, etc.) since that would imply that anyone who had ever been circumcised even as a child was now in opposition to the law. See Jewett, 'The Agitators and the Galatian Congregation', 202.

62 E. De W. Burton, *A Critical and Exegetical Commentary on the Epistle to the Galatians*, 353.

63 *Ibid.*, 353f.

64 Jewett, 'The Agitators and the Galatian Congregation', 202–3.

65 See W. W. Goodwin, *Greek Grammar*, 266; H. W. Smyth, *Greek Grammar*, 392.

66 For references see F. Blass and A. Debrunner, *A Greek Grammar of the New Testament and Other Early Christian Literature*, 166; A. T. Robertson, *A Grammar of the Greek New Testament in the Light of Historical Research*, 808–9.

67 The latter point needs emphasis for it is not just the independence of Paul that is at stake in the traditional view, for anyone could be independent of the apostles simply by rejecting their authority. Rather it is independence plus full apostolic recognition that is at stake.

68 Schmithals, *Paul & the Gnostics*, 19.

69 Whether it was 14 years after his conversion or 14 years after his first visit is difficult to tell.

70 Cf. J. Knox, *Chapters in a Life of Paul*, 52–3.

71 Lightfoot, *Galatians*, 350.

72 Baur, *Paul*, I, 124–7.

73 Munck, *Paul and the Salvation of Mankind*, 94. Bring, *Galatians*, 82, also

says that the text implies that Peter accepted Paul's rebuke.

74 Munck, *Paul and the Salvation of Mankind,* 100–2. T. Zahn, *Der Brief des Paulus an die Galater,* 112ff., held a similar view but for different reasons.

75 H. Feld, ' "Christus Diener der Sünde". Zum Ausgang des Streites zwischen Petrus und Paulus', *TQ,* 153 (1973), 119–31, holds that Gal. 2: 15–21 is Paul's strongest argument in demonstration of independence and moreover implies that Paul destroyed Peter's counter reasoning.

76 G. Bornkamm, *Paul,* 47, says that Paul's silence about the outcome of the clash 'can only mean that not he, but the others who were ready to give in to the strict Jewish Christians, won the day'.

77 See J. Dupont, 'Pierre et Paul à Antioche et à Jérusalem', *RSR,* 45 (1957), 42–60; 225–39, who criticizes attempts to change the order of events. For the problem which an unchronological narrative (lacking any note of explanation) would create within accepted rhetorical principles of Paul's day see H. D. Betz, 'The Literary Composition and Function of Paul's Letter to the Galatians', *NTS,* 21 (1975), 366f.

78 F. J. A. Hort, *Judaistic Christianity,* 77.

79 F. F. Bruce, 'Galatian Problems 1. Autobiographical Data', *BJRL,* 51 (1968–9), 308.

80 Schoeps, *Paul,* 68.

81 W. Schmithals, *Paul and James,* 65.

82 *Ibid.,* 65–7.

83 *Ibid.,* 72.

84 It is remarkable that some deny that Paul accuses Peter of 'compelling' Gentiles to be circumcised. See W. L. Knox, *St Paul and the Church of Jerusalem,* 196 n. 4; Schmithals, *Paul and James,* 69.

85 Lightfoot, *Galatians,* 354.

86 Hort, *Judaistic Christianity,* 78.

87 Schmithals, *Paul and James,* 69.

88 G. S. Duncan, *The Epistle of Paul to the Galatians,* 61.

89 The imperfects, ὑπέστελλεν and ἀφώριζεν, refer to a gradual withdrawal (see Burton, *Galatians* 107) which would have lent itself to ample opportunity for explanation and discussion.

90 F. F. Bruce, 'Galatian Problems 3. The "Other" Gospel', *BJRL,* 53 (1970–1), 257.

91 Schmithals, *Paul and James,* 72.

92 Whether 'those of the circumcision' (τοὺς ἐκ περιτομῆς) refers to the Jews as the cause of Peter's fear, as Schmithals contends (Schmithals, *Paul and James,* 66–8), or to the Jewish Christians in Jerusalem, is of little consequence for the present discussion. In either case Peter's actions reflect theological motivation catalyzed by fear.

93 This contrast is not weakened by the argument that the agreement envisioned that Jews and Gentiles would remain separate. The agreement in fact envisioned a mixture of the two in that it sanctioned Paul and Barnabas, two Jews, to be leaders of the Gentile mission.

94 Burton, *Galatians,* 76, says that the aorist ἠναγκάσθη in the present context implies that effort was exerted to compel Titus to be circumcised but was unsuccessful. If Paul had wished to imply that no effort toward compulsion was made he could have used the explicit imperfect with οὐκ. See

also Duncan, *Galatians,* 42: 'Another proposed interpretation of the verse according to which it means that "no pressure was ever applied to get Titus circumcised" is inconsistent with the Greek, and may be dismissed.'

95 Some have argued that Titus was in fact circumcised even though he was not compelled to do so. See F. C. Burkitt, *Christian Beginnings,* 118: 'Who can doubt that it was the knife which really did circumcise Titus that has cut the syntax of Gal. ii. 3–5 to pieces?' In our judgment the notion that Paul allowed a non-compulsory operation of circumcision on Titus is inconsistent with the apostle's irrevocable prohibition of circumcision to the Galatians. The fact that there was ample reason for a 'practical' circumcision among all the Gentiles, namely, to solidify the unity of the church, strongly suggests that Paul's absolute prohibition of it involved theological issues. Furthermore, since Paul's expression, οὐδέ... ἠναγκάσθη, implies an unsuccessful attempt at compulsion in the first place (see previous note), it seems highly unlikely that Paul would intend to convey to his readers, by the same words, that Titus after all was circumcised. What kind of victory would it have been for Paul, if after out-arguing the 'pillar' apostles over the circumcision of Titus, he had him circumcised anyway? To have written to the Galatians about circumcision in this manner would have been hopelessly confusing.

96 On this point see D. M. Hay, 'Paul's Indifference to Authority', *JBL,* 88 (1969), 36–44, who argues that Paul would not have continued to recognize their apostleship if their decision had been against the truth of the gospel. (See especially p. 42.)

97 T. W. Manson, 'St. Paul in Ephesus: (2) The Problem of the Epistle to the Galatians', *BJRL,* 24 (1940), 66.

98 Schmithals, *Paul and James,* 38–62.

99 Some think that Agabus' prophecy in Acts 11: 27–30 is parallel to this divine command. See most recently S. G. Wilson, *The Gentiles and the Gentile Mission in Luke-Acts,* 183.

100 Schmithals, *Paul and James,* 43.

101 O. Cullmann, *Peter. Disciple-Apostle-Martyr,* 18; 'Πέτρος, Κηφᾶς', *TDNT,* VI, 100.

102 E. Dinkler, *Signum Crucis,* 270–82; 'Die Petrus-Rom-Frage', *TR,* 25 (1959), 189–230.

103 G. Klein, 'Galater 2: 6–9 und die Geschichte der Jerusalemer Urgemeinde', *ZTK,* 57 (1960), 283–4.

104 Against this view see U. Wilckens, 'Der Ursprung der Überlieferung der Erscheinungen des Auferstandenen', *Dogma und Denkstrukturen,* 272 n.41.

105 Schmithals, *Paul and James,* 50.

106 See V. C. Pfitzner, *Paul and the Agon Motif. Traditional Athletic Imagery in the Pauline Literature,* 100: 'The context of the passage is as follows. Paul's work in the Galatian congregations is threatened with disruption through the work of legalists who in particular maintain that circumcision (Gal. 5: 2f., 6: 12f.) and the observation of cultic times and seasons (Gal. 4: 10) is still necessary for salvation.'

107 Schmithals, *Paul and James,* 65.

108 It is remarkable that later Schmithals himself recognizes the danger in the Jerusalem church accepting the contribution from Paul and the Gentiles

because of the possible punitive repercussions this might bring from the Jewish authorities; *Paul and James*, 79–84.

109 *Ibid.*, 65.

110 The position stated here and in what follows places the connection between 1 Cor. 15: 1ff. and Gal. 1: 11–12 in a non-opposing relationship in a way different from what others have tried. For another point of view see J. T. Sanders, 'Paul's "Autobiographical" Statements in Galatians 1–2', *JBL*, 85 (1966), 335–43.

111 If this interpretation is correct an apparent conflict exists between the text here and Acts 10, the so-called beginning of the Gentile mission, which in Acts goes to the credit of Peter. However, Paul's conversion is recorded in Acts 9, before the Cornelius episode and there is no indication that he told Peter or anyone else of his unique charge at that time. More-over, Luke's method of composition, i.e., of relating simultaneous periods of time in consecutive order (cf. Acts 8: 1 and 11: 19) makes it possible for the events of Acts 8: 4 – 11: 18 to be simultaneous with those of Acts 11: 19 – 14: 28. If this is so, it is possible to argue that the first missionary tour came before the Cornelius incident and that the events are recorded in their present order only to serve Luke's style and purpose of writing. See the suggestive remarks of Wilson, *The Gentiles and the Gentile Mission in Luke–Acts*, 151–2: 'Thus we should probably assume that 11: 19f. refers to a time prior to chs. 10–11 at least.' Cf. C. S. C. Williams, *A Commentary on the Acts of the Apostles*; 141.

112 The debate over whether James was an apostle is now famous. See espec-ially W. Schmithals, *The Office of Apostle in the Early Church*, 64–5.

113 Cf. Jos. *Ant.* 8. 46; *Bell.* 6. 81.

114 See the interesting article of G. D. Kilpatrick, 'Galatians 1: 18 ΙΣΤΟΡΗΣΑΙ ΚΗΦΑΝ', in *New Testament Essays. Studies in Memory of Thomas Walter Manson*, 144–9. Kilpatrick concludes that ἱστορῆσαι Κηφᾶν means 'to get information from Cephas'. W. D. Davies thinks ἱστορῆσαι may translate an Aramaic term denoting 'to seek after a tradition' or 'to inquire after a tradi-tion' or 'to visit an authoritative teacher'. See *The Gospel and the Land. Early Christianity and Jewish Territorial Doctrine*, 198.

115 E. Haenchen, 'The Book of Acts as Source Material for the History of Early Christianity', in *Studies in Luke–Acts*, 269, says: 'Only one thing is certain: Paul did not, at that time in Jerusalem, introduce himself as *the* apostle to the Gentiles, who preached Christianity without the Torah to the Gentiles and who claimed equality with Peter. They would most likely only have shaken their heads at such claims. In any case, if all this had then been dis-cussed and agreed upon, the later negotiations between Antioch and Jeru-salem would have been altogether unnecessary.'

116 See the remarks of John Knox on this point; J. Knox, *Chapters in a Life of Paul*, 37.

117 See H. Lietzmann, *An Die Galater*, 9.

118 We disagree with L. P. Trudinger, ' ἭΤΕΡΟΝ ΔΕ ΤΩΝ ΑΠΟΣΤΟΛΩΝ ΟΥΚ ΕΙΔΟΝ: ΕΙ ΜΗ ΙΑΚΩΒΟΝ A Note on Galatians i 19', *NT*, 17 (1975), 200–2, who translates Gal. 1: 19: 'Other *than* the apostles I saw none except James, the Lord's brother.' He gives a comparative force to ἕτερον and illustrates the construction with two examples from classical literature,

i.e., Th. 1. 28 and *De Mundo* (spuriously accredited to Aristotle). But
neither of these examples bears out the meaning which he ascribes to Gal.
1: 19. In each case ἕτερος is used to make a comparison between persons
or objects of the same class of things. In the first instance the Corcyraeans
could have been forced 'to make friends other [ἐτέρους] *than* those they
now had', and in the second Ether is described as 'being an element other
[ἕτερον] *than* the four'. In the first instance ἐτέρους refers to other *friends*
and in the second ἕτερον refers to another *element.* Thus in both cases the
persons or object belong to the same class of things as those with which
they are compared. If we make these examples analogous to Gal. 1: 19 it
follows that ἕτερον is *another apostle*, namely, James. It is possible, however, to use ἕτερον to distinguish between objects coming from
different classes of things. For example one may say 'a man is something
other than a horse or a rock', i.e., ἕτερον δὲ ἀνὴρ ἵππου ἢ πέτρας. In this
instance ἕτερον is unambiguously neuter, in no way modifying the nomina-
tive masculine ἀνήρ. For an example of this usage from classical literature
see Plato *Prot.* 333a: ἕτερον εἶναι σωφροσύνης σοφία. One may also acquire
this meaning by using ἕτερος in combination with παρά, ἤ, or
the dative case, e.g., Arist. *Pol.* 1294ᵃ 25 ὅτι μὲν οὖν ἐστὶ καὶ ἕτερα πολι-
τείας εἴδη παρὰ μοναρχίαν τε καὶ δημοκρατίαν καὶ ὀλιγαρχίαν. See also
Xen. *Cyr.* 1. 6. 2 and Diog. Laert. 3. 53. In Gal. 1: 19 ἕτερον is the masculine accusative object of εἶδον resulting in the literal translation: 'But other
of the apostles I saw not, except James.' Paul perhaps could have expressed
Trudinger's meaning as: ἕτερον δὲ ἢ τοὺ ἀποστόλους οὐκ εἶδον, εἰ Ἰάκωβον.

119   As we have seen Schmithals uses this as a key to understanding the entire
context; *supra*, 30–31. Bring, *Galatians,* 59, says that Paul uses these words
apparently to refute 'a claim by the Judaizers that he had been requested
to give an account of his activity by the leaders in Jerusalem and had been
reprimanded by them'.

120   Κατά with the accusative often means: 'on account of', 'in accordance
with', 'because of', 'in reference to', and even 'for the purpose of'. For
references see Bauer-Arndt-Gingrich, s.v. κατά II. 4, 5 δ.

121   A. Oepke, s.v. καλύπτω, *TDNT*, III, 585, says that 'it is on the basis of an
ἀποκόλυψις answer after the manner of Ac. 16: 9f' that Paul goes up to
Jerusalem on this occasion. But in Acts 16: 9, it is on the basis of a ὅραμα
(vision), not an ἀποκαλύφις, that Paul is called into Macedonia.

122   See Bornkamm, *Paul,* 21, who says that the word 'revelation' in Gal. 1:
15–16 and throughout Galatians 'means an objective world-changing event
through which God in his sovereign action has inaugurated a new aeon'.
His remark on p. 37, however, is inconsistent with this.

123   In all probability the Peshitta Version attempts to make this interpretation by
incorporating a play on the word *gly* into its translation: 'But I went up by revelation (*begelyana*) and I revealed (*waglith*) to them the gospel which I was
preaching among the Gentiles', i.e., 'I went up to make the revelation known.'

124   For a thorough discussion of Paul's reference to the 'pillar' apostles see τοῖς
δοκοῦσιν, etc., see C. K. Barrett, 'Paul and the "Pillar" Apostles' in *Studia
Paulina: in Honorem Johannis De Zwaan Septuagenarii,* 1–19.

125   O. Pfleiderer, *Primitive Christianity. Its Writings and Teachings in Their
Historical Connections,* I, 112.

126   See A. C. Bouquet, *Everyday Life in New Testament Times,* 120–2.

127　For a discussion of the possibilities see Burton, *Galatians*, 79–82. Cf. also
　　　B. Orchard, 'The Ellipsis between Galatians 2, 3 and 2, 4', *Biblica*, 54
　　　(1973), 469–81, and the reaction by A. C. M. Blommerde, 'Is there an
　　　Ellipsis between Galatians 2, 3 and 2, 4?' *Biblica*, 56 (1975), 100–2.
128　Duncan, *Galatians*, 43, says that Gal. 5: 11 suggests that Paul did have
　　　Titus circumcised, though not because he was compelled to do so.
　　　Duncan's reasoning, however, is based on the assumption, which we deny,
　　　that Paul's discussion in the autobiographical section aims at proving his
　　　independence of the Jerusalem leaders. In our judgment, 5: 11 is more
　　　easily explained on the basis that the judaizers out of ignorance actually
　　　thought that Paul practiced circumcision and considered him to be an
　　　ally, not an enemy; see the discussion in Chapter 1.
129　J. H. Schütz, *Paul and the Anatomy of Apostolic Authority*, 151, says:
　　　'Did both Jerusalem and Paul fail to foresee *at that time* the implications
　　　of recognizing an independent missionary movement based in Antioch? If
　　　Jerusalem could foresee such problems, was it acting in deception at the
　　　time of the meeting? Why would Barnabas, the most visible member of
　　　the Antioch missionary movement, succumb so quickly to Jerusalem's
　　　position if Jerusalem but reneged on an earlier agreement?' The fact is the
　　　Antioch crisis reflects a state of confusion on the part of Peter and Barna-
　　　bas only, of those involved in the Jerusalem meeting. Furthermore they
　　　did not renege arbitrarily, but rather out of ambivalent theological convic-
　　　tion. Barnabas obviously based his actions on his belief in the authority of
　　　Peter as the standard for theological truth. With Paul, on the other hand,
　　　the 'truth of the gospel' had been revealed to him by Christ. This gave him
　　　the stability, which Barnabas lacked, to tell Peter that his theology was
　　　deficient and imperfect. Paul's silence on James' position is very significant
　　　and may suggest that he was closer to Paul than Peter, contrary to what is
　　　often supposed, and that Peter's actions possibly were motivated by a mis-
　　　understanding of James' intent.
130　For more on this point see Chapter 4.
131　Or 'a certain one'; see Manson, 'St. Paul in Ephesus: (2)', 69–71.
132　Schmithals, *Paul and James*, 66ff.
133　William Neil says: 'Paul could not have challenged Peter openly as he did
　　　had he not been sure that basically Peter and he were of one heart and
　　　mind on the matter. What he was objecting to was Peter's temporary
　　　agreement for reasons of expediency with a policy in which neither he nor
　　　Paul believed.' W. Neil, *The Letter of Paul to the Galatians*, 41.
134　The play on the word ἁμαρτωλοί is clear. Cf. Jub. 23: 23–4.
135　On this point see G. Wagner, 'Le repas du Seigneur et la justification par la
　　　foi. Exégèse de Galates 2: 17', *ETR*, 36 (1961), 245–54.
136　This line of reasoning greatly mitigates the thesis that the judaizers were
　　　delegates from the Jerusalem church sent out to alter Paul's gospel of free-
　　　dom. Cf. most recently A. Strobel, 'Das Aposteldekret in Galatien: Zur
　　　Situation von Gal I und II', *NTS*, 20 (1974), 177–90.
137　See Chapter 1.
138　Though we do not agree with Schütz' interpretation of this passage, he is
　　　right in affirming that the first two chapters of Galatians are polemic, not
　　　apology. 'Hence it is safer to drop the presumption of apology in these

first two chapters and view them instead as Pauline polemic, as aggressive explication rather than defensive response.' Schütz, *Paul and the Anatomy of Apostolic Authority*, 128. H. D. Betz, 'Spirit, Freedom, and Law. Paul's Message to the Galatian Churches', *SEA*, 39 (1974), 155–6, says that Galatians is an 'apology'; he then explains, however, that Paul, in his strategy, 'is not at all defensive, but is rather on the attack'.

139   If Funk is right in his theory, based on formal grounds, that the apostolic letter was a substitute or surrogate for the charismatic and eschatological apostolic *parousia* (though somewhat less effective), Paul had reason to expect his letter to the Galatians to solve their problem. See R. W. Funk, 'The Apostolic *Parousia*: Form and Significance', in *Christian History and Interpretation: Studies Presented to John Knox*, 263–8. J. L. White likewise suggests that Galatians is a surrogate for Paul's apostolic presence, which could not itself take place because of a current imprisonment. He cites Gal. 5: 11 as possible evidence. See J. L. White, *The Body of the Greek Letter*, 110–11.

140   See C. K. Barrett, 'Paul's Opponents in II Corinthians', *NTS*, 17 (1970–1), 233–54 (especially 253–4).

141   Cf. Lightfoot, *Galatians*, 129.

142   Though perhaps not until some time after Paul penned Galatians.

143   Baur, *Paul*, I, 254–5.

144   *Ibid.*, 255.

145   Schmithals, *Paul & the Gnostics*, 41–3.

146   *Ibid.*, 41.

147   Bligh, *Galatians: A Discussion of St Paul's Epistle*, 173, 225, 235f.

148   R. W. Funk, *Language, Hermeneutic, and Word of God*, 262. He argues that Paul's letters have a form which aids in understanding both his own letters and the epistolary tradition in the early church.

149   White, *The Body of the Greek Letter*. See also his *The Form & Structure of the Official Petition: A Study in Greek Epistolography*.

150   White, *The Body of the Greek Letter*, 87f. Cf. also 73ff.

151   Betz, 'The Literary Composition and Function of Paul's Letter to the Galatians', 353–79. For a review of current studies in ancient rhetoric see G. Kennedy, 'Review Article: The Present State of the Study of Ancient Rhetoric', *CP*, 70 (1975), 278–82.

152   Cicero, *de Inventione* I. xiv. 19–liii. 100.

153   See F. Solmsen, 'Aristotle and Cicero on the Orator's Playing upon the Feelings', *CP*, 33 (1938), 390–404.

154   R. Bultmann, *Der Stil der paulinischen Predigt und die kynisch-stoische Diatribe*. It is also clear that Paul often followed Jewish / Rabbinic methods of interpretation. This will be discussed later.

155   Schoeps, *Paul*, 175–83.

156   *Ibid.*, 176.

157   H. D. McDonald, *Freedom in Faith: A Commentary on Paul's Epistle to the Galatians.*

158   *Ibid.*, 70.

159   *Ibid.*

160   *Ibid.*, 72.

161   *Ibid.*, 73.

162   *Ibid.*, 74.

163   *Ibid.*, 77.

164   See J. B. Phillips' translation of Rom. 3: 27 in *Letters to Young Churches*, 9.

165   Schoeps, *Paul*, 66.

166   Bruce, 'Galatian Problems 3', 263.

167   McDonald, *Freedom in Faith*, 54.

168   Lightfoot, *Galatians*, 312.

169   'The preaching of Jesus as the Christ of Scripture could not be believed by Jews if His followers left the Law of God. Hereby the community and its Head would be condemned from the very outset in their eyes.' See W. Gutbrod, s.v. νόμος, *TDNT*, IV, 1067. W. D. Davies says that Paul continued to keep the law without demanding the Gentiles to keep it in order to be true to the 'new' and the 'old' Israel. Moreover, he says it was expedient for Paul to keep the law himself in order to keep the avenues of communication open between himself and Rabbinic Judaism. W. D. Davies, *Paul and Rabbinic Judaism*, 69–74.

170   Cf. Chapter 2,

171   B. Lindars, *New Testament Apologetic. The Doctrinal Significance of the Old Testament Quotations*, 229.

172   Bligh, *Galatians: A Discussion of St Paul's Epistle*, 257f. Cf. also H. Hübner, 'Gal 3: 10 und die Herkunft des Paulus', *KUD*, 19 (1973), 215–31, who traces Paul's strict understanding of the law's demands back to a Shammaite Pharisaical background.

173   James 2: 10 spurs the people on to greater vigilance in keeping the law by arguing that one is guilty of the whole law if he stumbles in one point. But James does not say, nor does he imply, that one sin is the end of the line with no possible means of forgiveness.

174   The International Organization for Septuagint and Cognate Studies came into being in 1968 and now publishes an annual *Bulletin* that lists work currently being done in the field. See also the recent book by S. Jellicoe, *The Septuagint and Modern Study*.

175   A new Targum studies group is now included among affiliated groups under the Society of Biblical Literature umbrella. Its first *Newsletter* appeared January 1974.

176   On the meaning of midrash see R. Le Déaut, 'Apropos a Definition of Midrash', *Interpretation*, 25 (1971), 259–82.

177   The concept of the New Testament writers adopting *ad hoc* readings or adjusting their quotations of the Old Testament to fit their particular point of view has been discussed at length in recent times. Among the most helpful works are: K. Stendahl, *The School of St. Matthew and Its Use of the Old Testament*; see especially his remarks in the Introduction of the new edition in light of the developments in Old Testament recensional criticism based on the views of Barthélemy and Cross. E. E. Ellis, *Paul's Use of the Old Testament*; 'A Note on Pauline Hermeneutics', *NTS*, 2 (1955–6), 127–33; F. F. Bruce, *Biblical Exegesis in the Qumran Texts*; J. A. Fitzmyer, 'The Use of Explicit Old Testament Quotations in Qumran Literature and

in the New Testament', *NTS*, 7 (1960–1), 297–333; Lindars, *New Testament Apologetic*; M. P. Miller, 'Targum, Midrash and the Use of the Old Testament in the New Testament', *JSJ*, 2 (1971), 29–83; D. M. Smith, Jr., 'The Use of the Old Testament in the New', in *The Use of the Old Testament in the New and Other Essays: Studies in Honor of William Franklin Stinespring*, 3–65.

178   This is succinctly stated by Tasker: 'To have faith similar to Abraham's faith is also to inherit the blessing promised to him and to his seed.' See R. V. G. Tasker, *The Old Testament in the New Testament*, 96. Cf. also Burton, *Galatians*, 155: 'The unexpressed premise of this argument is that men become acceptable to God and heirs of the promise on the same basis on which Abraham himself was accepted.'

179   Lindars, *New Testament Apologetic*, 225.

180   1 Macc. 2: 51–2; Philo *de Abrahamo* 262–76, *de Virtutibus* 214–19; Mechilta on Exodus XIV. 31. See also James 2: 21–4 which cites the same passage and concludes that Abraham's faith plus his works was the basis of his justification. Although one might assume that even in justification by faith only, faith must have at least a small grain of merit, it is argued that Paul thought of faith as absolutely unmeritorious. Thus Fitzmyer says that 'the faith of the Christian is a gift of God just as the whole salvific process'. See J. A. Fitzmyer, *Pauline Theology: A Brief Sketch*, 64. Later he says that faith is actually man's response to God.

181   On this point see especially E. Jacob, 'Abraham et sa signification pour la foi chrétienne', *RHPR*, 42 (1962), 148–56.

182   See McDonald, *Freedom in Faith*, 69; Duncan, *Galatians*, 84f.

183   For an analysis of possible different perspectives in the role of Abraham and the law in Rom. 4 and Gal. 3 see K. Berger, 'Abraham in den paulinischen Hauptbriefen', *MTZ*, 17 (1966), 47–89.

184   See D. J. Doughty, 'The Priority of XAΡΙΣ. An Investigation of the Theological Language of Paul', *NTS*, 19 (1972–3), 166, who wrestles with 'Paul's own *presupposition* for his interpretation of πίστις in such a way as to exclude every appeal to human accomplishment'. This to Doughty is totally foreign to the common Jewish understanding of Abraham's faith which was meritorious.

185   See E. De W. Burton, *Syntax of the Moods and Tenses in New Testament Greek*, 102.

186   Cf. W. Sanday and A. C. Headlam, *A Critical and Exegetical Commentary on the Epistle to the Romans*, 100, who say: 'St. Paul does not question the supposed claim that Abraham has a καύχημα absolutely – before man he might have it and the Jews were not wrong in the veneration with which they regarded his memory – but it was another thing to have a καύχημα before God.'

187   See H. Schlier, *Der Brief an die Galater*, 128. See also the full treatment of this subject in H.-W. Heidland, *Die Anrechnung des Glaubens zur Gerechtigkeit*, especially 119–23. On p. 121 he says: 'Deshalb muss das λογίζεσθαι des Zitats ein Anrechnen κατὰ χάριν, eine "Gnadengabe" sein, und steht im Gegensatz zu einem Anrechnen κατὰ ὀφείλημα, einer "Pflichtgabe".' See also H.-W. Heidland, s.v. λογίζομαι, λογισμός in *TDNT*, IV, 284–92. In our judgment J. A. Ziesler, *The Meaning of Righteousness in Paul. A*

Linguistic and Theological Enquiry is wrong in rejecting Heidland's view
that Paul interprets Gen. 15: 6 as an act of pure grace on God's part apart
from any intrinsic value in Abraham's faith.

188 Cf. Gal. 3: 6, 18.

189 Davies, *The Gospel and the Land*, 172, suggests that Paul's combination of
Gen. 15: 6 and Ps. 32: 1–2 was legitimate because of the technical exegetical
device of *gezerah shawa*, which permitted the connection of two passages
using the same term (in this case λογίζεσθαι) for purposes of interpretation.

190 We find a similar juxtaposing of the word πίστις and its cognates in Rom. 3:
3 (ἠπίστησαν... ἀπιστία... πίστιν) and Gal. 2: 16 (πίστεως... ἐπιστεύσαμεν
...πίστεως). Cf. also Philo *de Abrahamo* 273: 'That God marvelling at
Abraham's faith [πίστεως] in Him repaid him with faithfulness [πίστιν]
by confirming with an oath the gifts which He had promised' (Loeb translation).

191 I have dealt at length with the 'faith of Christ' in other publications and
refer the reader to them for details and further bibliography. See G. Howard,
'Notes and Observations on the "Faith of Christ" ' *HTR*, 60 (1967), 459–65;
G. Howard, 'The "Faith of Christ",' *ET*, 85 (1974), 212–15. A brief summary of the data gathered to date is offered here. The phrase πίστις
Χριστοῦ (or its equivalent) occurs eight or nine times in the Pauline corpus
(viz., Rom. 3: 22, 26; Gal. 2: 16 (twice), 2: 20, 3: 22, (3: 26 in P⁴⁶); Eph.
3: 12; Philip. 3: 9). Arguments in favor of the subjective genitive (viz.,
'faith *of* Christ') are: (1) In Hellenistic Jewish Literature πίστις is rarely,
if ever, followed by the non-subjective personal genitive. Lührmann
describes the genitive in Jos. *Ant.* 17. 284, ἐπὶ δεξιαῖς καὶ πίστει τοῦ θείου,
as puzzling. See D. Lührmann, 'Pistis im Judentum', *ZNW*, 64 (1973), 28.
R. Marcus' translation in the Loeb edition (VIII, 505): 'On receiving a
pledge sworn by his faith in God', is doubtful. It is better to translate:
'Upon receiving assurances and a pledge (sworn) in the name of God.' Cf.
Th. 5. 30: θεῶν γὰρ πίστεις ὀμόσαντες ἐκείνοις οὐκ ἂν εὐορκεῖν προδι-
δόντες αὐτούς, 'having sworn to them with pledges by the gods, it would
not be consistent with the oath to give them up'.) When the writers wish
to express the notion of faith *in* someone they employ the preposition,
e.g., τὴν πρὸς τὸν θεὸν πίστιν (Philo *Mut.* 201). (2) The Latin Vulgate, the
Peshitta Syriac, and the Sahidic Coptic all render the phrase either literally
or make the subjective genitive explicitly clear. Thus the Latin is always
fides Christi, and the Coptic *tpistis m̄pechs̄*, both meaning literally 'faith
of Christ'. The Peshitta renders the phrase either *haymanutha dameshiha*,
'faith of the Messiah' or *haymanutheh dameshiha*, 'his faith, namely, that
of the Messiah'. In the latter instance the meaning is explicitly 'the Messiah's
faith'. In addition all three versions clearly distinguish this concept from the
notion of 'faith *in* Christ' by use of other constructions.

Luther seems to have been the first to give the objective genitival meaning to the phrase, usually rendering it *Glaube an Christum*; (see, however,
his rendition of Gal. 2: 20). Other versions of the Reformation period,
however, retained the meaning of the subjective genitive. Thus the Author-
ized Version of 1611 always (except for Rom. 3: 26) renders the phrase
'faith of Christ' and the old Spanish version of Casiodoro de Reine revised
by Ciprano de Valera in 1602 translates *la fe de Cristo*. In light of this data

the preponderant weight of evidence suggests that πίστις Χριστοῦ means 'the faith of Christ'.

192 Lindars, *New Testament Apologetic*, 235.

193 See Lightfoot, *Galatians*, 139; Bandstra, *The Law and the Elements*, 124; Duncan, *Galatians*, 99; Lietzmann, *Galater*, 19.

194 D. W. B. Robinson, 'The Distinction Between Jewish and Gentile Believers in Galatians', *ABR*, 13 (1965), 34. Bligh, as we have seen, argues that this whole section was taken from Paul's Antioch speech which was delivered to Jews not Gentiles. See Bligh, *Galatians: A Discussion of St Paul's Epistle*, 257f.

195 Burton, *Galatians*, 164, 168, argues that the curse is the universal judgment of the principle of legalism. Therefore redemption from it is release from the false notion that God deals with man on the basis of legalism. Bring, *Galatians*, 143f., is unclear in his presentation. He says that the law applied primarily to the Jews but Paul understood Israel to represent all men because all had sinned. Later he says that Christ's redemption from the curse of the law was a redemption of everyone since all men were under some law (p. 146). W. L. Knox, *St Paul and the Church of the Gentiles*, 108, says that the 'Torah brought a curse on all who disobeyed it; since no man could obey it, it brought a curse on all men'. Later he says that Christ liberated from the curse and the consequent subjection to the Torah 'those who had been plunged into matter by the sin of their first parent'.

196 R. T. Stamm, 'The Epistle to the Galatians', *The Interpreter's Bible*, X, 505. See also more recently Tyson, ' "Works of Law" in Galatians', 428.

197 Cf. Reicke, 'The Law and this World', 274 n. 49: 'Notice that *everyone* who does not obey this commandment is damned according to v. 10. Paul is interested chiefly in the Judaizers, and it is really for this reason that he lays the emphasis on πᾶς, but this makes it apparent that the heathen are also included.'

198 Bandstra, *The Law and the Elements*, 59–62, argues that a distinction should be made in the pronouns. His theory will be stated more fully in the next chapter.

199 For an explanation of Rom. 10: 4 see G. Howard, 'Christ the End of the Law: The Meaning of Romans 10: 4ff.', *JBL*, 88 (1969), 331–7. My conclusion is that Christ is the goal (*telos*) of the law to everyone who believes in the sense that he achieved the goal of the law by ushering the Gentiles into the kingdom of God.

200 Thus we disagree with C. Haufe, 'Die Stellung des Paulus zum Gesetz', *TL*, 91 (1966), 171–8, who argues that in Pauline thought the cultic-ceremonial law had been done away, but not its moral imperative.

201 In the next chapter this point will be developed further to show that disunity in mankind was tantamount to polytheism in Paul's mind.

202 In Chapter 1 we argued that Paul considered being under the law tantamount to being in the flesh. For an explanation of how the view above harmonizes with that position see *supra*, Chapter 1 n. 48.

203 Davies, *The Gospel and the Land*, 179. See also McEleney, 'Conversion, Circumcision and the Law', 340.

204 Therefore we agree partially with the words of Bandstra, *The Law and the Elements*, 124: 'It was just *because* Paul recognized the validity of the law

given to Israel as a mark of Israel's priority, that he insisted that the law, which at the same time separated Israel and the Gentiles, had to be set aside and negated. It was only when the law, the source of the enmity between Jew and Greek, had been set aside in Christ that the unity of all men in Him could be established. This unity was to come about through the principle of faith, for it was given to Abraham by the earlier promise so that he could be the father of all believers, and it was rooted in the One God of both Jews and Gentiles.'

205 On the dividing force of the law see U. Mauser, 'Galater iii. 20: Die Universalität des Heils', *NTS,* 13 (1967), 258–70.

206 Thus Paul says: 'For if the inheritance is by the law it is no longer by promise' (Gal. 3: 18); 'For if those out of law are heirs, the faith is emptied, and the promise is made invalid' (Rom. 4: 14).

207 Gal. 2: 21 seems to suggest that some considered the law as the grace (χάρις) of God. Paul assures them that it is not.

208 C. H. Dodd thinks that Hab. 2: 3–4 may have belonged to a traditional *testimonium* used by the early church. If so Paul's choice of Scripture here was probably one which was commonly accepted both by him and his opponents. See Dodd, *According to the Scriptures,* 49–51.

209 T. W. Manson argues that *LXX* gives a messianic interpretation which is further messianized by the writer of the Epistle to the Hebrews. See Manson, 'The Argument from Prophecy', *JTS,* 46 (1945–6), 129–36. See also Lindars, *New Testament Apologetic,* 230f.

210 See Zahn, *Der Brief des Paulus an die Galater,* 155.

211 J. A. Sanders, 'Habakkuk in Qumran, Paul, and the Old Testament', *JR,* 39 (1959), 233. See also W. H. Brownlee, 'Messianic Motifs of Qumran and the New Testament', *NTS,* 3 (1956–7), 209.

212 F. F. Bruce, 'Qumrân and Early Christianity', *NTS,* 2 (1955–6), 183.

213 *Ibid.*

214 Lightfoot, *Galatians,* 139.

215 Schlier, *Galater,* 134.

216 F. Mussner, *Der Galaterbrief,* 231.

217 Cf. J. J. O'Rourke, 'Pistis in Romans', *CBQ,* 35 (1973), 188–94. On p. 194 he says: 'If even some of the proposed interpretations of the use of *pistis* in Rom. be correct, Paul stresses even more than has been usually thought God's part in man's justification.'

218 On this point see in particular E. Bammel, 'Gottes *diathēkē* (Gal. iii. 15–17) und das Jüdische Rechtsdenken', *NTS,* 6 (1960), 313–19.

219 It is best to understand διὰ τῆς πίστεως ἐν Χριστῷ Ἰησοῦ (vs. 26) as meaning: 'Through this faith (which resides) in Christ', viz., 'Christ's faith'. P[46], which reads πίστεως Χριστοῦ Ἰησοῦ, preserves either the original wording of the text or expresses an ancient interpretation. This reading is supported by the Peshitta Syriac and the Sahidic Coptic. Similar constructions are: 1 Tim. 1: 14 (πίστεως καὶ ἀγάπης τῆς ἐν Χριστῷ Ἰησοῦ), 2 Tim. 2: 1 (ἐν τῇ χάριτι τῇ ἐν Χριστῷ Ἰησοῦ). Cf. the discussions in Mussner, *Galaterbrief,* 261f. and S. Légasse, 'Foi et baptême chez saint Paul: Étude de Galates 3, 26–7', *BLE,* 74 (1973), 81–102.

220 Among the growing literature some of the most helpful are the following: H. Diels, *Elementum. Eine Vorarbeit zum griechischen und lateinischen*

Thesaurus; M. Dibelius, *Die Geisterwelt im Glauben des Paulus;* F. Pfister, 'Die στοιχεῖα τοῦ κόσμου in den Briefen des Apostels Paulus', *Philologus,* 69 (N.S.) 23 (1910), 411–27; O. Lagercrantz, *Elementum: Eine lexikologische Studie;* Burton, *Galatians,* 510–18; C. Blum, 'The Meaning of στοιχεῖον and its Derivates in the Byzantine Age. A Study in Byzantine Magic', *Eranos,* 44 (1946), 315–25; W. Burkert, 'ΣΤΟΙΧΕΙΟΝ Eine semasiologische Studie', *Philologus,* 102–3 (1958–9), 167–97; Bandstra, *The Law and the Elements;* G. Delling, s.v. στοιχεῖον, *TDNT,* VII, 670–87. For a recent survey of representative interpretations see especially Mussner, *Galaterbrief,* 293–7.

221 See also Philo, *Vita Mosis* I, 96. This is against Duncan, *Galatians,* 134, who says that besides Gal. 4: 3, Col. 2: 8, 20, τὰ στοιχεῖα τοῦ κόσμου in this exact form occurs nowhere else in Greek literature. See Lietzmann, *Galater,* 24–6 for a good brief discussion of this phrase.

222 The association of τὰ στοιχεῖα τοῦ κόσμου in Col. 2: 6–15 with τὰς ἀρχάς and τὰς ἐξουσίας points in the same direction.

223 A. W. Cramer, *Stoicheia tou Kosmou,* 37–42, 59, 60; Bandstra, *The Law and the Elements,* 43–4 ('In the first place, the earliest unmistakable evidence for the word in question meaning "spirits" or "demons" is *The Testament of Solomon,* which in its present form is post-Christian and may not be earlier than the third or fourth century.' 44); Delling, 'στοιχεῖον', 684–5. See also Zahn, *Der Brief des Paulus an die Galater,* 197–8.

224 Thus Isa. 37: 19 οὐ γὰρ θεοὶ ἦσαν ἀλλὰ ἔργα χειρῶν ἀνθρώπων; Jer. 2: 11 καὶ οὗτοι οὐκ εἰσιν θεοί; 5: 7 ὤμνυον ἐν τοῖς οὐκ οὖσιν θεοῖς; 16: 20 καὶ οὗτοι οὐκ εἰσιν Θεοί; also especially see the numerous satirical references in Ep. Jer. 14, 22, 28, 49, 50, 64, 68, 71.

225 Neil, *Galatians,* 63.

226 Bligh, *Galatians: A Discussion of St Paul's Epistle,* 330–1.

227 *Ibid.,* 330.

228 *Ibid.,* 331.

229 *Ibid.,* 334.

230 Bandstra, *The Law and the Elements,* 59–62.

231 *Ibid.,* 60. See also Cramer, *Stoicheia Tou Kosmou,* 126–9, for a similar view.

232 Bandstra, *The Law and the Elements,* 55.

233 *Ibid.,* 65–7.

234 Schlier, *Galater,* 193.

235 Reicke, 'The Law and this World', 259–76.

236 *Ibid.,* 274–5.

237 *Ibid.,* 268.

238 G. B. Caird, *Principalities and Powers. A Study in Pauline Theology.*

239 *Ibid.,* 47–8.

240 *Ibid.,* 49.

241 *Ibid.,* 51.

242 Reicke, 'The Law and this World', 273–4, makes an attempt to place the Gentiles under the Torah, but at the same time he explains that the Gentiles knew what God's requirements were from the law of nature. Although he apparently senses that Paul viewed the Gentiles as actually under the law

of Moses he fails to distinguish this clearly from his point about the law of
nature. See also Bandstra, *The Law and the Elements*, 64. Mussner, *Galaterbrief*, 192, seems to hold that the Gentiles knew the law only from the
voice of conscience. In his comment on Gal. 3: 11 (pp. 228–9) he says that
' "law" is stretched: the Torah becomes, as it were, a "world law", by which
no one is justified, a thing which is valid for every time (present δικαιοῦαι)
not only for the time before Christ'.

243   Burton, *Galatians*, 216, 219, 518.
244   Neil, *Galatians*, 64.
245   Lightfoot, *Galatians*, 173. It should be noted that Lightfoot is careful also
      to point out those characteristics of paganism which separate it from Juda-
      ism. See also H. A. W. Meyer, *Critical and Exegetical Hand-Book to the
      Epistle to the Galatians*, 168–9.
246   R. Leivestad, *Christ the Conqueror. Ideas of Conflict and Victory in the
      New Testament*, 95f.
247   Burton, *Galatians*, 231; Schlier, *Galater*, 203 n. 1, says: 'The στοιχεῖα are
      ἀσθενῆ probably in the sense of Col. 2: 15, Eph. 1: 21; πτωχά in regard
      to the fact that they can bring no life or have no heirs.'
248   As we have seen Reicke, Bandstra and Mussner attempt it. Cf. *supra*, n. 242.
249   Again Reicke, 'The Law and this World', 274–5, attempts to do this by
      arguing that 1 Cor. 10: 20 teaches that Israel in its sacrifices makes offerings
      to demons. There are variant readings within the manuscript tradition, how-
      ever, which, if original, make this passage refer to Gentiles only. He also
      cites 2 Cor. 4: 4 and Philip. 3: 18ff. Bligh, *Galatians: A Discussion of St
      Paul's Epistle*, 339, perhaps approaches the notion that Judaism is paganistic
      when he says: 'A crass material like circumcision, for example, belongs
      to the same crude level of religious observance as the self-castration of
      Phrygian priests alluded to in 5: 12.' Mussner, *Galaterbrief*, 302, says that
      Paul warns the Galatians against acceptance of calendar-piety because of
      the danger of this leading into a superstitious star worship.
250   Lightfoot, *Galatians*, 173.
251   Cf. the remarks of E. Käsemann, *Perspectives on Paul*, 72, who denies that
      Paul ever 'detached the ritual from the ethical law'.
252   Bring, *Galatians*, 190.
253   Caird, *Principalities and Powers*, 49.
254   Cf. in general B. Reicke, 'Natürliche Theologie nach Paulus', *SEA*, 22–3
      (1957–8), 154–67; J. L. McKenzie, 'Natural Law in the New Testament',
      BR, 9 (1964), 3–13.
255   Caird, *Principalities and Powers*, 49.
256   *Ibid.*, 50–1.
257   *Ibid.*, 41.
258   In later times, of course, it was believed that man could find release from
      fate through the practice of cultic and magical rites. See Knox, *St Paul and
      the Church of the Gentiles*, 101; F. Cumont, *Astrology and Religion among
      the Greeks and Romans*, 17–18.
259   A general misunderstanding of the legalistic aspects of the law is corrected
      by E. P. Sanders, 'Patterns of Religion in Paul and Rabbinic Judaism: A
      Holistic Method of Comparison', *HTR*, 66 (1973), 455–78; especially
      458–66.

260   See Howard, 'Romans 3: 21-31 and the Inclusion of the Gentiles'.
261   See Howard, 'Christ the End of the Law: The Meaning of Romans 10:4ff.'.
262   Cf. Acts 7: 53; Heb. 2: 2; Jub. 1: 27, Philo *de Somniis* I, 141-3; Jos. *Ant.*
       15. 136. On the last reference see W. D. Davies, 'A Note on Josephus,
       Antiquities 15. 136', *HTR*, 47 (1954), 135-40.
263   See for example 2 Enoch 34: 1-2; Jub. 11: 2-6.
264   In general see F. Cumont, *Oriental Religions in Roman Paganism.*
265   For a more complete discussion of the Intertestamental Jewish position on
       Gentile religion see D. S. Russell, *The Method and Message of Jewish
       Apocalyptic,* 235ff.
266   Gustaf Aulén's now famous book, *Christus Victor,* describes the Classic
       View of Atonement in terms of Christ's victory over the Devil in the
       resurrection.
267   Bring, *Galatians,* 82. Lightfoot, *Galatians,* 112, says that they may have been
       invested with some powers from James which they abused.
268   This, of course, is in opposition to Cullmann, *Peter,* 50-1, 65.
269   On this particular point see Ropes, *Singular Problem,* 6.
270   Paul says in Gal. 3: 28 that there is neither Jew nor Greek, bond nor free,
       male nor female. This is true in so far as they are 'in Christ'. But in the
       present world he knew that racial, sexual, and class distinctions would in
       actual fact continue, and in the case of Israel's distinctiveness, it was
       significant for God's salvific purposes.
271   Lightfoot, *Galatians,* 365, 371f.

BIBLIOGRAPHY

Aland, K., et al. *The Greek New Testament. Stuttgart:* United Bible
  Societies, 1966.
Aristotle. *Politica.* Oxford Classical Texts. Edited by D. Ross. Oxford:
  Clarendon Press, 1957.
Aulén, G. *Christus Victor.* Macmillan Co., r.p. 1969.
Bammel. E. 'Gottes *diathēkē* (Gal. iii. 15–17) und das Jüdische Rechts-
  denken'. *NTS,* 6 (1960), 313–19.
Bandstra, A. J. *The Law and the Elements of the World. An Exegetical
  Study in Aspects of Paul's Teaching.* Grand Rapids: Wm. B.
  Eerdmans, 1964.
Barrett, C. K. 'Paul and the "Pillar" Apostles'. *Studia Paulina in Honorem
  Johannis De Zwaan Septuagenarii.* Edited by J. N. Sevenster and
  W. C. van Unnik. Haarlem: De Erven F. Bohn N.V., 1953.
'Paul's Opponents in II Corinthians'. *NTS,* 17 (1970–71), 233–54.
'Pauline Controversies in the Post-Pauline Period'. *NTS,* 20 (1974),
  229–45.
Barth, M. 'The Kerygma of Galatians', *Interpretation,* 21 (1967), 131–46.
Barthélemy, D. *Les devanciers d'Aquila.* Leiden: E. J. Brill, 1963.
Bauer, W.; Arndt, W.; and Gingrich, F. W. *A Greek-English Lexicon of the
  New Testament and Other Early Christian Literature.* Cambridge:
  University Press, 1957.
Bauernfeind, O. 'Die Begegnung zwischen Paulus und Kephas, Gal 1: 18–
  20.' *ZNW,* 47 (1956), 268–76.
Baur, F. C. 'Die Christuspartei in der korinthischen Gemeinde, der Gegen-
  satz des petrinischen und paulinischen Christenthums in der ältesten
  Kirche, der Apostel Petrus im Rom'. *Tübinger Zeitschrift für
  Theologie,* V: 4 (1831), 61–206.
*Paul the Apostle of Jesus Christ, His Life and Work, His Epistles and
  His Doctrine. A Contribution to a Critical History of Primitive
  Christianity.* 2 volumes. Translated by E. Zeller. 2nd ed. London:
  Williams and Norgate, 1876.
Berger, K. 'Abraham in den paulinischen Hauptbriefen'. *MTZ,* 17 (1966),
  47–89.
Betz, H. D. 'Spirit, Freedom, and Law. Paul's Message to the Galatian
  Churches'. *SEA,* 39 (1974), 145–60.
'The Literary Composition and Function of Paul's Letter to the
  Galatians'. *NTS,* 21 (1975), 353–79.

The Holy Bible. Revised Standard Version. New York: Thomas Nelson and Sons, 1952.

Blass, F. and Debrunner, A. *A Greek Grammar of the New Testament and Other Early Christian Literature.* Revised and translated by R. W. Funk. Chicago: University of Chicago Press, 1961.

Bligh, J. *Galatians in Greek.* Detroit: University of Detroit Press, 1966.
Galatians: A Discussion of St Paul's Epistle. London: St Paul Publications, 1969.

Blommerde, A. C. M. 'Is There an Ellipsis between Galatians 2, 3 and 2, 4?' *Biblica,* 56 (1975), 100-2.

Blum, C. 'The Meaning of στοιχεῖον and its Derivates in the Byzantine Age. A Study in Byzantine Magic'. *Eranos,* 44 (1946), 315-25.

Bornkamm, G. *Paul.* Translated by D. M. G. Stalker. London: Hodder and Stoughton, 1971.

Bouquet, A. C. *Everyday Life in New Testament Times.* New York: Charles Scribner's Sons, 1954.

Bring, R. *Commentary on Galatians.* Translated by E. Wahlstrom. Philadelphia: Muhlenberg Press, 1961.

Brownlee, W. H. 'Messianic Motifs of Qumran and the New Testament'. *NTS,* 3 (1956-7), 195-210.

Bruce, F. F. 'Qumrân and Early Christianity'. *NTS,* 2 (1955-6), 176-90.
Biblical Exegesis in the Qumran Texts. London: Tyndale Press, 1959.
'Galatian Problems 1. Autobiographical Data'. *BJRL,* 51 (1969), 292-309.
'Galatian Problems 3. The "Other" Gospel', *BJRL,* 53 (1970-71), 253-71.

Bultmann, R. *Der Stil der paulinischen Predigt und die kynisch-Stoische Diatribe.* Forschungen zur Religion und Literatur des Alten und Neuen Testaments 13; Göttingen: Vandenhoeck und Ruprecht, 1910.

Burkert, W. 'ΣΤΟΙΧΕΙΟΝ. Eine semasiologische Studie'. *Philologus,* 102-3 (1958-9), 167-97.

Burkitt, F. C. *Christian Beginnings.* London: University of London Press, 1924.

Burrows, M., Trever, J. C. and Brownlee, W. H., editors. *The Dead Sea Scrolls of St. Mark's Monastery. Volume I. The Isaiah Manuscript and the Habakkuk Commentary.* New Haven: The American Schools of Oriental Research, 1950.

Burton, E. De W. *Syntax of the Moods and Tenses in New Testament Greek.* 3rd ed. Edinburgh: T. and T. Clark, 1898.
A Critical and Exegetical Commentary on the Epistle to the Galatians. ICC; New York: Charles Scribner's Sons, 1920.

Caird, G. B. *Principalities and Powers. A Study in Pauline Theology.* Oxford: Clarendon Press, 1956.

Cicero, Marcus Tullius. *de Inventione.* Translated by H. M. Hubbell. Loeb Classical Library; Cambridge: Harvard University Press, 1949.

Conzelmann, H. *History of Primitive Christianity.* Nashville: Abingdon Press, 1973.

Cramer, A. W. *Stoicheia tou Kosmou.* Kieuwkoop: de Graaf, 1961.

Crownfield, F. R. 'The Singular Problem of the Dual Galatians'. *JBL,* 63

(1945), 491–500.
Cullmann, O. *Peter. Disciple–Apostle–Martyr*. Translated by F. V. Filson. London: SCM Press, 1953.
'Πέτρος, Κηφᾶς'. *TDNT*, VI, 100–12.
Cumont, F. *Oriental Religions in Roman Paganism*. New York: Dover Publications, r.p. 1956.
Astrology and Religion among the Greeks and Romanι New York: Dover Publications, r.p. 1960.
Davies, W. D. 'A Note on Josephus, Antiquities 15. 136'. *HTR*, 47 (1954), 135–40.
Paul and Rabbinic Judaism. 2nd ed. London: SPCK, 1965.
The Gospel and the Land. Early Christianity and Jewish Territorial Doctrine. Berkeley: University of California Press, 1974.
Delling, G. 'στοιχεῖον'. *TDNT*, VII, 670–87.
Dibelius, M. *Die Geisterwelt im Glauben des Paulus*. Göttingen: Vandenhoeck und Ruprecht, 1909.
Diels, H. *Elementum. Eine Vorarbeit zum griechischen und lateinischen Thesaurus*. Leipzig, 1899.
Dinkler, E. 'Die Petrus–Rom–Frage'. *TR*, 25 (1959), 189–230.
Signum Crucis. Tübingen, 1967.
Diogenes Laertius, *Lives of Eminent Philosophers*. 2 volumes. Translated by R. H. Hicks. Loeb Classical Library; New York: G. P. Putnam's Sons, 1925.
Dodd, C. H. *According to the Scriptures*. London: Nisbet and Co., Ltd., 1952.
Doughty, D. J. 'The Priority of ΧΑΡΙΣ. An Investigation of the Theological Language of Paul'. *NTS*, 19 (1972–3), 163–80.
Duncan, G. S. *The Epistle of Paul to the Galatians*. Moffatt Series; New York: Harper and Brothers, preface dated 1934.
Dupont, J. 'Pierre et Paul à Antioche et à Jérusalem'. *RSR*, 45 (1957), 42–60; 225–39.
Ellis, E. E. 'A Note on Pauline Hermeneutics'. *NTS*, 2 (1955–6), 127–33.
Paul's Use of the Old Testament. Grand Rapids: Eerdmans, 1957.
Feld, H. ' "Christus Diener der Sünde". Zum Ausgang des Streites zwischen Petrus und Paulus'. *TQ*, 153 (1973), 119–31.
Fitzmyer, J. A. 'The Use of Explicit Old Testament Quotations in Qumran Literature and in the New Testament'. *NTS*, 7 (1961), 297–333.
Pauline Theology: A Brief Sketch. Englewood Cliffs: Prentice-Hall, 1967.
Funk, R. W. *Language, Hermeneutic, and Word of God*. New York: Harper and Row, 1966.
'The Apostolic *Parousia*: Form and Significance'. *Christian History and Interpretation: Studies Presented to John Knox*. Edited by W. R. Farmer, C. F. D. Moule, and R. R. Niebuhr. Cambridge: University Press, 1967.
Geiger, W. *Spekulation und Kritik: Die Geschichtstheologie Ferdinand Christian Baurs*. München: Chr. Kaiser Verlag, 1964.
Goodwin, W. W. *Greek Grammar*. Revised by C. B. Gulick. New York: Ginn and Co., 1930.
Gunther, J. J. *St. Paul's Opponents and Their Background: A Study of*

Apocalyptic and Jewish Sectarian Teachings. Leiden: E. J. Brill, 1973.

Gutbrod, W. s.v. 'νόμος'. *TDNT*, IV, 1036-1091.

Haenchen, E. 'The Book of Acts as Source Material for the History of Early Christianity'. *Studies in Luke-Acts.* Edited by L. E. Keck and J. L. Martyn. Nashville: Abingdon Press, 1966.

Haufe, C. 'Die Stellung des Paulus zum Gesetz'. *TL*, 91 (1966), 171-8.

Hay, D. M. 'Paul's Indifference to Authority'. *JBL*, 88 (1969), 36-44.

Heidland, H.-W. *Die Anrechnung des Glaubens zur Gerechtigkeit.* Stuttgart: W. Kohlhammer, 1936.

'λογίξομαι, λογισμός'. *TDNT*, IV, 284-92.

Hirsch, E. 'Zwei Fragen zu Galater 6'. *ZNW*, 29 (1930), 192-7.

Hodgson, P. C. *The Formation of Historical Theology.* New York: Harper and Row, 1966.

Holtzmann, O. 'Zu Emanuel Hirsch, Zwei Fragen zu Galater 6'. *ZNW*, 30 (1931), 76-83.

Hort, F. J. A. *Judaistic Christianity.* London: Macmillan and Co., 1904.

Howard, G. 'Notes and Observations on the "Faith of Christ" '. *HTR*, 60 (1967), 459-65.

'Christ the End of the Law: The Meaning of Romans 10: 4ff'. *JBL*, 88 (1969), 331-7.

'The "Faith of Christ" ', *ET*, 85 (1974), 212-15.

Hübner, H. 'Gal 3: 10 und die Herkunft des Paulus'. *KUD*, 19 (1973), 215-31.

Jacob, E. 'Abraham et sa signification pour la foi chrétienne'. *RHPR*, 42 (1962), 148-56.

Jellicoe, S. *The Septuagint and Modern Study.* Oxford: Clarendon Press, 1968.

Jewett, R. 'The Agitators and the Galatian Congregation'. *NTS*, 17 (1971), 198-212.

Paul's Anthropological Terms. A Study of Their Use in Conflict Settings. Leiden: E. J. Brill, 1971.

Josephus Flavius. *Opera.* 7 volumes. Edited by Benedictus Niese. Berlin: Weidmann, 1955.

Käsemann, E. *Perspectives on Paul.* Philadelphia: Fortress Press, 1971.

Kennedy, G. 'Review Article: The Present State of the Study of Ancient Rhetoric'. *CP*, 70 (1975), 278-82.

Kilpatrick, G. D. 'Galatians 1: 18 ΙΣΤΟΡΗΣΑΙ ΚΗΦΑΝ', *New Testament Essays. Studies in Memory of Thomas Walter Manson.* Edited by A. J. B. Higgins. Manchester: University of Manchester Press, 1959.

Kittel, *Biblia Hebraica.* Stuttgart: Privilegierte Württembergische Bibel-anstalt, 1935.

Klein, G. 'Galater 2: 6-9 und die Geschichte der Jerusalemer Urgemeinde'. *ZTK*, 57 (1960), 275-95.

Klijn, A. F. J. 'The Study of Jewish Christianity'. *NTS*, 20 (1974), 419-31.

Knox, J. *Chapters in a Life of Paul.* Nashville: Abingdon-Cokesbury Press, 1950.

Knox, W. L. *St Paul and the Church of Jerusalem.* Cambridge: University Press, 1925.

St Paul and the Church of the Gentiles. Cambridge: University Press, 1939.

Kümmel, W. G. *The New Testament: The History of the Investigation of Its Problems.* Translated by S. M. Gilmour and H. C. Kee. Nashville: Abingdon Press, 1972.

Lagercrantz, O. *Elementum: Eine lexikologische Studie.* Uppsala-Leipzig, 1911.

Le Déaut, R. 'Apropos a Definition of Midrash'. *Interpretation,* 25 (1971), 259–82.

Légasse, S. 'Foi et baptême chez saint Paul: Étude de Galates 3, 26–7. *BLE,* 74 (1973), 81–102.

Leivestad, R. *Christ the Conqueror. Ideas of Conflict and Victory in the New Testament.* London: SPCK, 1954.

Lietzmann, H. *An Die Galater.* 3rd ed. Tübingen: J. C. B. Mohr, 1932.

Lightfoot, J. B. *St Paul's Epistle to the Galatians.* 6th ed. London: Macmillan and Co., 1880.

Lindars, B. *New Testament Apologetic. The Doctrinal Significance of the Old Testament Quotations.* London: SCM Press Ltd., 1961.

Lohse, E. *Die Texte Aus Qumran.* Darmstadt: Wissenschaftliche Buchgesellschaft, 1964.

Lührmann, D. 'Pistis im Judentum'. *ZNW,* 64 (1973), 19–38.

Lütgert, W. *Gesetz und Geist: Eine Untersuchung zur Vorgeschichte des Galaterbriefes.* Gütersloh: Druck und Verlag von Bertelsmann, 1919.

McDonald, H. D. *Freedom in Faith. A Commentary on Paul's Epistle to the Galatians.* London: Pickering and Inglis Ltd., 1973.

McEleney, N. J. 'Conversion, Circumcision and the Law'. *NTS,* 20 (1974), 319–41.

McKenzie, J. L. 'Natural Law in the New Testament'. *BR,* 9 (1964), 3–13.

Manson, T. W. 'St. Paul in Ephesus: (2) The Problem of the Epistle to the Galatians'. *BJRL,* 24 (1940), 59–80.

'The Argument from Prophecy'. *JTS,* 46 (1945–6), 129–36.

Mauser, U. 'Galater iii. 20: Die Universalität des Heils'. *NTS,* 13 (1967), 258–70.

Meyer, H. A. W. *Critical and Exegetical Hand-Book to the Epistle to the Galatians.* New York: Funk and Wagnalls, 1884.

Miller, M. P. 'Targum, Midrash and the Use of the Old Testament in the New Testament', *JSJ,* 2 (1971), 29–83.

Munck, J. *Paul and the Salvation of Mankind.* Translated by F. Clarke. Richmond: John Knox Press, 1959.

Mussner, F. *Der Galaterbrief.* Freiburg: Herder, 1974.

Neil, W. *The Letter of Paul to the Galatians.* CBC; Cambridge: University Press, 1967.

Oepke, A. 'καλύπτω'. *TDNT,* III, 556–92.

Orchard, B. 'The Ellipsis between Galatians 2, 3 and 2, 4'. *Biblica,* 54 (1973), 469–81.

O'Rourke, J. J. 'Pistis in Romans'. *CBQ,* 35 (1973), 188–94.

Pfister, F. 'Die στοιχεῖα τοῦ κόσμου in den Briefen des Apostels Paulus'.

Philologus, 69 (N.S.) 23 (1910), 411–27.

Pfitzner, V. C. *Paul and the Agon Motif. Traditional Athletic Imagery in the Pauline Literature.* Leiden: E. J. Brill, 1967.

Pfleiderer, O. *Primitive Christianity. Its Writings and Teachings in Their Historical Connections.* Translated by W. Montgomery. Clifton, N. J.: Reference Book Publishers, Inc., r.p. 1965. Volume I.

Phillips, J. B. *Letters to Young Churches.* New York: Macmillan Co., 1955.

Philonis Alexandrini opera quae supersunt. 6 volumes. Edited by L. Cohn and P. Wendland. Berlin: G. Reimer, 1896–1915. Indexes by J. Leisegang. 2 volumes. Berlin: de Gruyter, 1926–30.

Plato, *Protagoras.* Edited by J. Burnet. Oxford Classical Texts. Oxford: Clarendon Press, 1901, Volume III.

Rahlfs, A., editor. *Septuaginta id est Vetus Testamentum Graece iuxta LXX Interpretes.* 2 volumes. Editio Sexta; Stuttgart: Privilegierte Württembergische Bibelanstalt; n.d.

Ramsay, W. M. *The Church in the Roman Empire.* 5th ed. London: Hodder and Stoughton, 1897.

Reicke, B. 'The Law and this World According to Paul: Some Thoughts concerning Gal 4: 1–11'. *JBL,* 70 (1951), 259–76.

'Natürliche Theologie nach Paulus'. *SEA,* 22–3 (1957–8), 154–67.

Robertson, A. T. *A Grammar of the Greek New Testament in the Light of Historical Research.* Nashville: Broadman Press, 1934.

Robinson, D. W. B. 'The Distinction Between Jewish and Gentile Believers in Galatians'. *ABR,* 13 (1965), 29–48.

Ropes, J. H. *The Singular Problem of the Epistle to the Galatians.* Cambridge: Harvard University Press, 1929.

Russell, D. S. *The Method and Message of Jewish Apocalyptic.* Philadelphia: Westminster Press, 1964.

Sanday, W. and Headlam, A. C. *A Critical and Exegetical Commentary on the Epistle to the Romans.* 5th ed. ICC; Edinburgh: T. and T. Clark, 1907.

Sanders, E. P. 'Patterns of Religion in Paul and Rabbinic Judaism: A Holistic Method of Comparison'. *HTR,* 66 (1973), 455–78.

Sanders, J. A. 'Habakkuk in Qumran, Paul, and the Old Testament'. *JR,* 39 (1959), 232–44.

Sanders, J. T. 'Paul's "Autobiographical" Statements in Galatians 1–2'. *JBL,* 85 (1966), 335–43.

Schlier, H. *Der Brief an die Galater.* 13th ed. Göttingen: Vandenhoeck and Ruprecht, 1965.

Schmithals, W. *Paul and James.* SBT 46; Naperville, Ill.: Alec R. Allenson, 1965.

The Office of Apostle in the Early Church. Translated by J. E. Steely. Nashville: Abingdon Press, 1969.

Paul & the Gnostics. Translated by J. E. Steely. Nashville: Abingdon Press, 1972.

Schoeps, H. J. *Paul: The Theology of the Apostle in the Light of Jewish Religious History.* Translated by H. Knight. Philadelphia: Westminster Press, 1961.

Schütz, J. H. *Paul and the Anatomy of Apostolic Authority.* Cambridge:

University Press, 1975.

Selby, D. J. *Toward the Understanding of St. Paul.* Englewood Cliffs: Prentice-Hall, Inc., 1962.

Smith, D. M., Jr. 'The Use of the Old Testament in the New'. *The Use of the Old Testament in the New and Other Essays: Studies in Honor of William Franklin Stinespring.* Edited by J. M. Efrid. Durham: Duke University Press, 1972.

Smyth, H. W. *Greek Grammar.* Cambridge: Harvard University Press, 1956.

Solmsen, F. 'Aristotle and Cicero on the Orator's Playing upon the Feelings'. *CP,* 33 (1938), 390–404.

Stamm, R. T. 'The Epistle to the Galatians'. *The Interpreter's Bible.* New York: Abingdon-Cokesbury Press, 1953.

Stendahl, K. 'The Apostle Paul and the Introspective Conscience of the West'. *HTR,* 56 (1963), 199–215.

The School of St. Matthew and Its Use of the Old Testament. New Edition; Philadelphia: Fortress Press, 1968.

Strobel, A. 'Das Aposteldekret in Galatien: Zur Situation von Gal I und II'. *NTS,* 20 (1974), 177–90.

Talbert, C. H. 'Again: Paul's Visits to Jerusalem'. *NT,* 9 (1967), 26–40.

Tasker, R. V. G. *The Old Testament in the New Testament.* Grand Rapids: Eerdmans, 1954.

Thucydides. *History of the Peloponnesian War.* 4 volumes. Translated by C. F. Smith. Loeb Classical Library; Cambridge: Harvard University Press, 1958.

Trudinger, L. P. ' "ΕΤΕΡΟΝ ΔΕ ΤΩΝ ΑΠΟΣΤΟΛΩΝ ΟΥΚ ΕΙΔΟΝ, ΕΙ ΜΗ ΙΑΚΩBON A Note on Galatians i 19'. *NT,* 17 (1975), 200–2.

Tyson, J. B. 'Paul's Opponents in Galatia'. *NT,* 10 (1968), 241–54.

' "Works of Law" in Galatians'. *JBL,* 92 (1973), 423–31.

Wagner, G. 'Le repas du Seigneur et la justification par la foi. Exégèse de Galates 2: 17'. *ETR,* 36 (1961), 245–54.

White, J. L. *The Form and Structure of the Official Petition: A Study in Greek Epistolography.* SBL Dissertation Series 5; Missoula, Montana: Society of Biblical Literature, 1972.

The Body of the Greek Letter. SBL Dissertation Series 2; Missoula, Montana: Society of Biblical Literature, 1972.

Wilckens, U. 'Der Ursprung der Überlieferung der Erscheinungen des Auferstandenen'. *Dogma und Denkstrukturen.* Göttingen, 1963.

Williams, C. S. C. *A Commentary on the Acts of the Apostles.* Harper's New Testament Commentaries; New York: Harper and Bros., 1957.

Wilson, R. McL. 'Gnostics – in Galatia?' *SE,* 4 (1968), 358–67 (= *TU* no. 102, 1968).

Wilson, S. G. *The Gentiles and the Gentile Mission in Luke-Acts.* Cambridge: University Press, 1973.

Xenophon. *Cyropaedia.* 2 volumes. Translated by Walter Miller. Loeb Classical Library; Cambridge: Harvard University Press, 1960–61.

Zahn, T. *Der Brief des Paulus an die Galater.* 3rd ed. Leipzig: A. Deichertsche Verlagsbuchhandlung, 1922.

Ziegler, J., editor. *Septuaginta Vetus Testamentum Graecum. XIII Duodecium Prophetae.* 2. Auflage; Göttingen: Vandenhoeck und

Ruprecht, 1967.
Ziesler, J. A. *The Meaning of Righteousness in Paul. A Linguistic and Theological Enquiry.* Cambridge: University Press, 1972.

INDEX OF SUBJECTS AND NAMES

INDEX OF PASSAGES QUOTED